The Complete Acoustic BLUES GUITAR METHOD
by Woody Mann

NEW REPERTOIRE FOR FINGERSTYLE BLUES GUITAR

To access audio visit:
www.halleonard.com/mylibrary

Enter Code
5298-0266-0296-1282

ISBN 978-1-78305-248-6

For all works contained herein:
Unauthorized copying, arranging, adapting, recording, Internet posting, public performance,
or other distribution of the music in this publication is an infringement of copyright.
Infringers are liable under the law.

Visit Hal Leonard Online at
www.halleonard.com

Contact us:
Hal Leonard
7777 West Bluemound Road
Milwaukee, WI 53213
Email: info@halleonard.com

In Europe, contact:
Hal Leonard Europe Limited
42 Wigmore Street
Marylebone, London, W1U 2RN
Email: info@halleonardeurope.com

In Australia, contact:
Hal Leonard Australia Pty. Ltd.
4 Lentara Court
Cheltenham, Victoria, 3192 Australia
Email: info@halleonard.com.au

This book © Copyright 2014 Wise Publications.

Unauthorised reproduction of any part of this publication by any
means including photocopying
is an infringement of copyright.

Written by Woody Mann
Edited by David Bradley
Book design by Fresh Lemon
Photo page 7 by Rod Franklin

Photographs courtesy of:
GAB Archive/Redferns,
Hulton Archive/Getty Images,
Michael Ochs Archives/Getty Images,
Frank Driggs Collection/Getty Images,
Tony Evans/Timelapse Library Ltd,
David Redfern/Redferns,
Rue des Archives/PVDE.

Music recorded, mixed and mastered by Woody Mann

All songs by Woody Mann
© 2014 Lee Haywood Studio Publishing (SESAC)
PO Box 903 Times Square Station, New York, NY 10018
All Rights Reserved

Dedicated to Robert Tilling

ACKNOWLEDGEMENTS

To Rev. Gary Davis for teaching me how to listen,
my mother for getting me to his house,
and my students who taught me how to teach.
Thanks to my good friend and guitarist
Pete McDonough for writing the artist biographies.

Woody Mann, NYC
www.woodymann.com
www.woodymannguitarlessons.com

CONTENTS

Introduction 6

Playing Acoustic Blues 8
The Rhythm; Picking Technique
Steady Bass 9

Creole Baby 11
Bye Bye Blues 14
Barrelhouse Blues 16
Syncopated Picking 18
Blues In A 19
Richard's Riff 22

The Music 24

Fingerstyle Blues Basics 26
John C's Rag 28
Good Feeling Blues 30
Ragtime Strut 32

Ragtime Syncopation 34
Durham Dance 36
Come On Boys 38
Black Cat Blues 40
Ragging The Blues 42
Do I Have To Wait? 44
East Coast Rag 46
Do Anything If You Let Me 48

Country Blues Styles 50
Lonesome Man Blues 52
Lordy Lord Blues 54
The Devil And Me 56
Baby Come Back 58
Little Vicksburg 60
Old Time Blues 62

Texas Nights 64
Mistreating Woman 66
Texarkana Valley 68
Highway Bound 70
River Blues 72
Papa Charlie's Blues 74
The Dirt Road 76
Bo's Blues 78
Mr. Jefferson's Blues 82

Open And Altered Tunings 84
Beale Street Rock 84
Tampa Blues 86
What's The Matter? 88
Good Girl 90
Big Road 92
Fandango In Open G 94
Skippy's Blues 96
Mississippi Moan 98
You Got To Know How 100
Blues Ain't Gone 102
Farewell Baby 105
Blues In G 108
Police Blues 110
Jump Blues 112

Expanding The Traditions 114
Sunday Church Meeting 114
Hudson River Boogie 116
Sunset Lake Rag 118
Spiritual For R.G.D. 120
Virginia Stomp 122
At Midnight 124
Delta Nights 126

INTRODUCTION

Acoustic blues is one of America's richest musical traditions. The artists who recorded in the 1920s and 1930s created a body of guitar work that, in many ways, established the basics of playing technique for traditional as well as many contemporary styles of acoustic fingerstyle guitar music. The early blues traditions developed through a combination of many musical influences, including country, gospel, pop, and folk music. Artists from all different geographic regions of the South and Midwest created their unique individual approaches to the guitar. The sounds, approaches, and techniques cover a wide range, including many song styles and structures that cannot be categorized.

My goal in this book is to teach a cross section of the playing styles of some of the most influential and popular artists, as well as the obscure (but no less great) players. There is no better way to learn the music than by going directly to the source. Learning from the original 78s, however, can be confusing. Because of the sound quality, improvised nature of the performances, and the vast array of styles and tunings, it can be difficult to grasp the basic ideas while also playing along. As the musicians are usually improvising, each verse is different, and their picking styles have so much variation it can also be confusing to figure out a way to approach learning it.

Instead of presenting a series of exercises or transcriptions of the original 78 rpm recordings, I decided to write original compositions based on the playing styles of the early masters. The approach is to learn blues guitar by playing blues guitar. Each tune is a clear and playable example of a particular style, artist, or recording. I have selected a cross section of styles that illustrate playing techniques in most of the keys and tunings. So, as you learn new repertoire, you will also build your technique. These new compositions illustrate the ideas in a graded way, in which I hope to provide a clear understanding of the craft.

Writing these instrumentals was a fun project. It gave me the freedom to present the music in a practical way. The 51 instrumentals I've written offer a wide variety of sounds and styles, ranging from the basics to more complicated playing techniques. The sounds cover the spectrum—from the stylized and syncopated sounds of ragtime blues, to the open tuning approaches of the Mississippi Delta, to the folk sounds of the Carolinas—while also featuring some of the most classic arrangements in acoustic blues. I also included a section called "Expanding the Traditions," which features new fingerstyle pieces that use the ideas of traditional blues to show how they can be applied to a more contemporary sound. Through these original songs, my goal is to take the beginner student from the basics of "how to pick" to more complex and sophisticated ideas and offer ideas for further exploration.

My own playing developed through many hours of trying to learn songs off the recordings. I was also lucky enough to take lessons with Reverend Gary Davis and to play with blues masters such as Son House and Bukka White. The overall lesson I learned time and again was always the same: sound, swing, and spontaneity make up the essence of the music. When I would learn a tune from Davis and go back for my next lesson, he would invariably play it differently. Needless to say this was very frustrating but, after a while, I realized that his subtle improvisations were simply part of the music.

There are many styles of blues and countless subtleties of technique. Although one book cannot cover it all, this collection is designed to provide the basics, and then some. In the song notes, I referenced the blues artist whose music that particular tune is based on. Hopefully, playing these instrumentals will inspire you to listen to the original artists and enable you to get into the music in a deeper way and learn directly from the original recordings.

PLAYING ACOUSTIC BLUES

THE RHYTHM (PICKING TECHNIQUE)

Acoustic blues may be a simple music to analyze but it can be difficult to play. The sound and subtleties of rhythm and dynamics are at the center of the music. The sound subtleties of rhythm and dynamics are everything. Achieving a good sound and being able to create variations in your own playing begins with having a relaxed and strong picking hand. This is what provides the swing and groove in the music, as well as where the ability to improvise begins. Understanding the basic mechanics of how you are playing a tune is as important as grasping what you are playing.

Even though the chords, riffs, and melodies are different in each tune, the picking approach connects them all. Understanding this overall fingerpicking idea will make it easier to play all the songs. Whether your favorite blues guitarist is Robert Johnson, Muddy Waters, Mississippi John Hurt, Big Bill Broonzy, Lonnie Johnson, Skip James, or Blind Blake, learning the basic ideas is a good first step toward being able to capture the essence of their traditional styles.

STEADY BASS

Many of the traditional acoustic blues guitar styles were developed by guitarists imitating the two-handed approach of the piano. Just as the pianist learned to play different parts with each hand—one for bass and the other for melody—the guitarist imitated this with the thumb and fingers of the picking hand. This basic two-line approach is common to all styles of acoustic blues playing. The bass line is played with your thumb, while the treble line is played with your fingers. I notated the music in two "voices" to illustrate these two lines. The melodies are written with up stems (played with your fingers), while the bass line is represented by down stems (played with your thumb). At first, the goal is to play a bass note on the beat with your thumb while playing a simple melody with your fingers. (In some cases the bass and melody crisscross where your fingers might be playing on the low strings.) The next step is to embellish both parts with rhythmic syncopations and melodic variations. The greater the independence, the easier it becomes to negotiate the syncopation and capture the swing and subtleties of the music. Rather than playing in patterns, think of the music as two independent lines—like playing the piano. The following songs illustrate the various ways this picking idea can be applied.

THE COMPLETE ACOUSTIC BLUES GUITAR METHOD

CREOLE BABY

In the first example, the picking is played with a steady alternating bass line, played as quarter notes against the rhythms in the melody. In each verse variation, the rhythm of the melody changes while the bass remains alternating on the beat. Achieving a smooth, relaxed, steady bass under a melody is a good first plateau to reach. This song is based on the playing of Mississippi John Hurt's "My Creole Belle."

Mississippi John Hurt

Mississippi John Hurt was born in 1892 as John Smith Hurt in Teoc, Mississippi. In 1928, he recorded a series of sides for the Okeh record label. As his recordings were met with little commercial success, Hurt continued to work as farmer and field laborer; as a musician, he fell into obscurity. In 1963, he was "rediscovered" and performed at the Newport Folk Festival. Hurt continued to play concerts at clubs and universities and record again until his death in 1966. Known for his melodic approach and alternating bass fingerpicking technique, he was inducted into the Blues Hall of Fame in 1988.

Standard tuning

Swing ($\sqcap = \sqcap^3$)

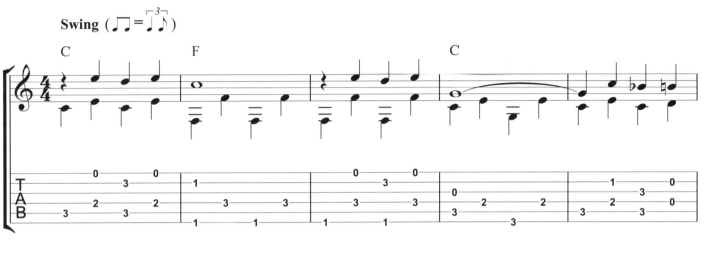
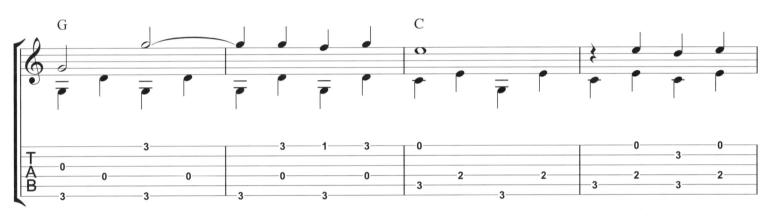
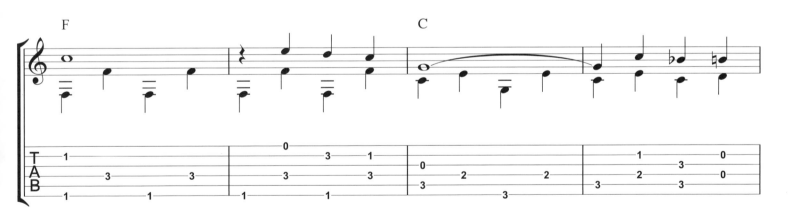
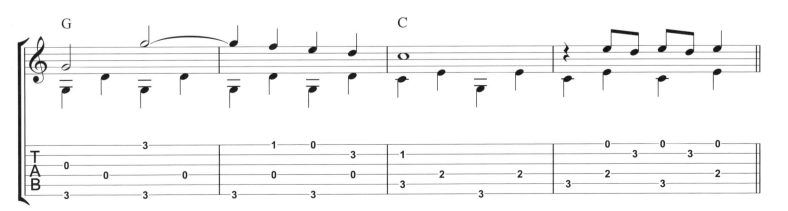

Variation 1

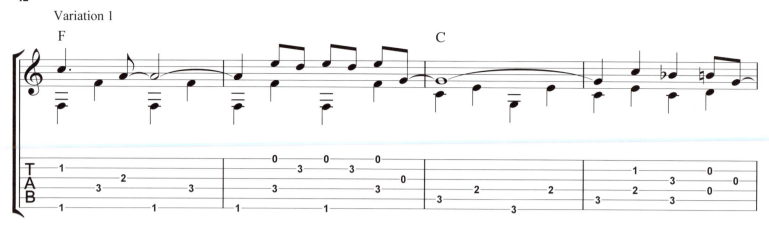
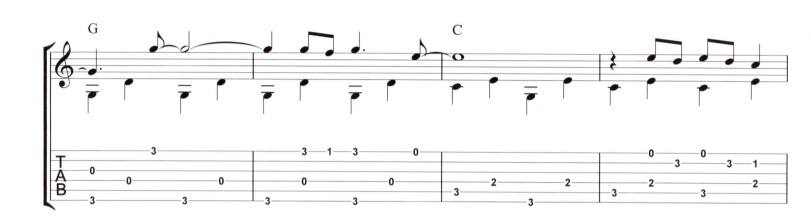
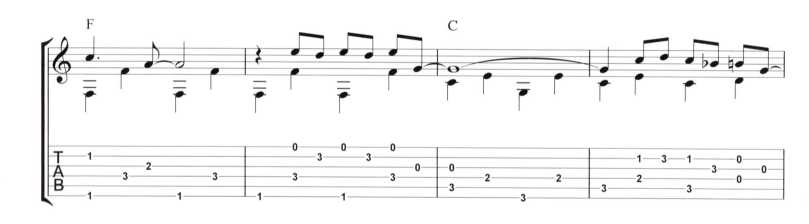
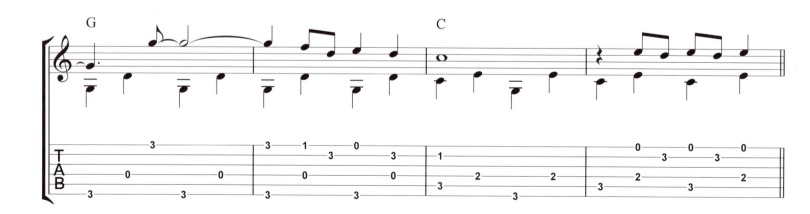

Variation 2

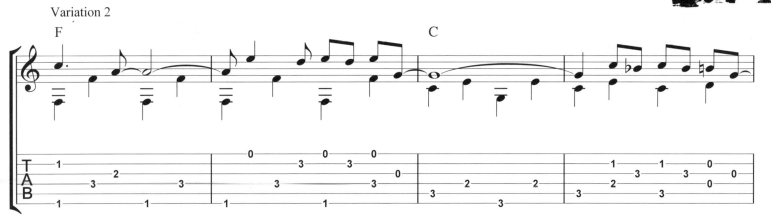
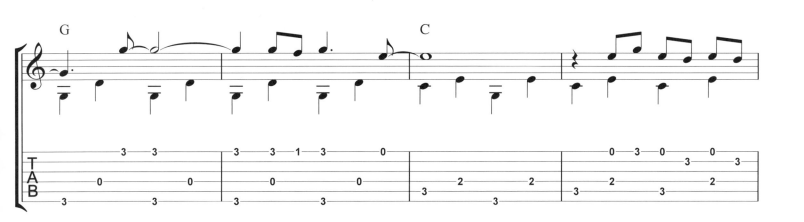
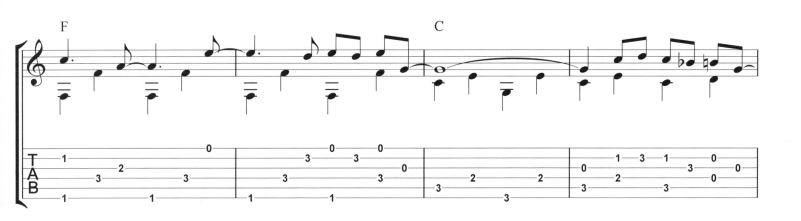
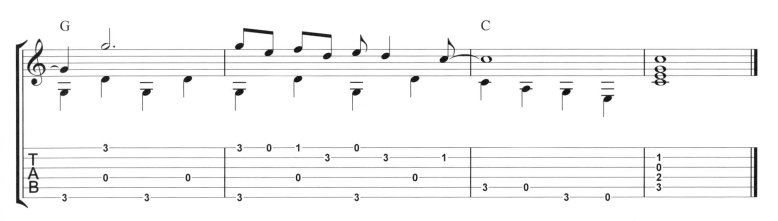

BYE BYE BLUES

Little Hat Jones

A Texas street-singer born in Bowie County, Texas, in 1899, George "Little Hat" Jones spent virtually all of his life in the Lone Star State. Jones's recordings were all made during three sessions over the course of 1929–1930, when he recorded twenty songs – eleven as a solo artist and nine accompanying Texas Alexander. Despite living for more than eighty years, Jones never recorded another song after the 1930 session. Little Hat Jones is best remembered for his tune "Bye Bye Baby Blues." He died in Naples, Texas, in 1981.

The next song is an example of a steady alternating bass line with some ideas on how to create variations in the melody. The tune is based on "Bye Bye Baby Blues," by the great blues guitarist Little Hat Jones. It is a beautiful and simple 16-bar folk melody played against a steady alternating bass. The first verse states the melody, and verses two and three are variations. Try playing more than one note at a time with your thumb by brushing the bass strings. This gives the song a strum-like feel and creates a fuller sound and a more rhythmic pulse to the alternating bass.

BARRELHOUSE BLUES

Memphis Minnie

Born Lizzie Douglas in Algiers, Louisiana, in 1897, Memphis Minnie became one of the most prolific and gifted female blues guitar players and singers. Douglas ran away from home in her early teens, joined the Ringling Brothers Circus, and first performed under the name Kid Douglas. She permanently adopted the stage name Memphis Minnie in the late 1920s.

Over the course of her more than forty-year recording career, Memphis Minnie recorded more than 150 sides as a solo artist and more than 200 sides with two of her husbands. She became, in the early 1940s, one of the first blues artists to begin playing electric guitar. Minnie lived most of her life in Chicago, Detroit, and Indianapolis. She returned to Memphis in the late 1950s where she lived until her death in 1973.

"Barrelhouse Blues" is another example of a steady and alternating bass played under a more syncopated and chromatic melody line. The more rhythmic the melody, the more difficult it is to keep the bass on the beat. Once you feel comfortable with the picking, play the alternating bass with damping. The two verses are based on the playing of Memphis Minnie.

Standard tuning   Swing (♫ = ♩♪)

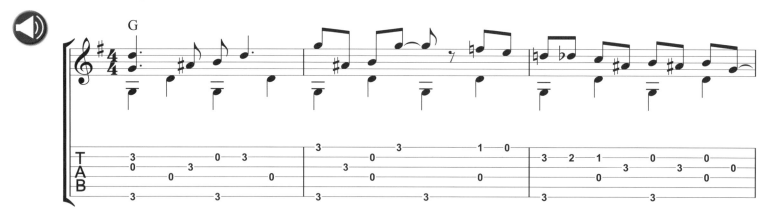

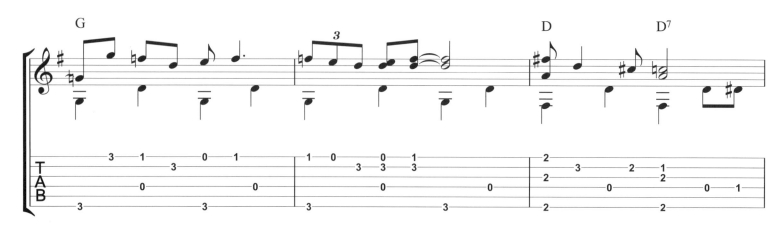

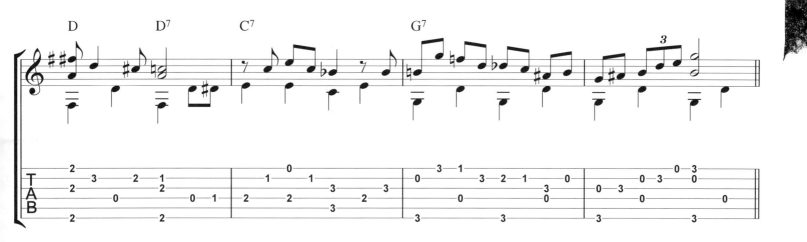

Verse 2

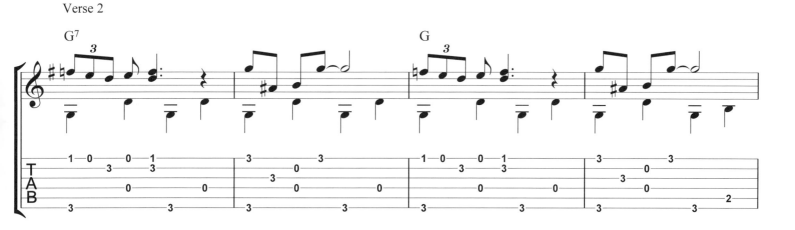

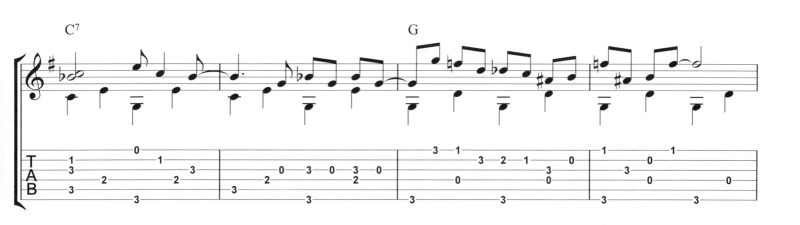

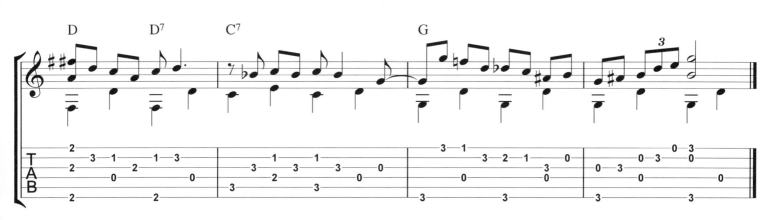

SYNCOPATED PICKING

Syncopated picking is one of the most important techniques to learn. Artists whose playing styles are very different—such as Blind Blake, Blind Lemon Jefferson, Robert Johnson, Son House, Scrapper Blackwell, Rev. Gary Davis, and Lonnie Johnson—are similar in that they all use syncopated picking in their music. Country blues guitar was originally played for dances. The rhythm of the dance comes from the syncopations and subtleties of the picking hand. Adding syncopation to your "toolbox" of picking techniques is essential for playing the subtleties of country blues.

BLUES IN A

To illustrate how to add different types of syncopation in the bass, I wrote out three verses of a 12-bar blues in the key of A. The first verse has a typical alternating bass with a simple melody. In the next two verses, I added the variations. The syncopated bass is played on the upbeats as well as the downbeats, creating a "bouncy," more rhythmic feel. This "double thumbing" or "drop thumb" technique is played by dragging your thumb across the bass strings from the upbeat into the downbeat of the next bass note—as in a rest stroke. Let your thumb move across the bass strings in one motion.

Standard tuning

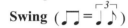

Verse 1

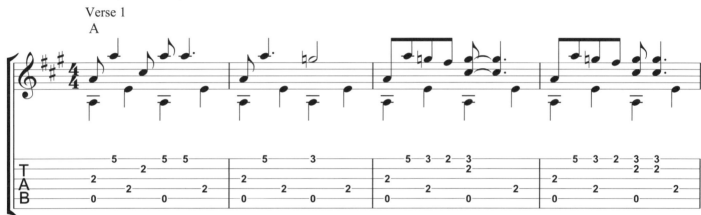

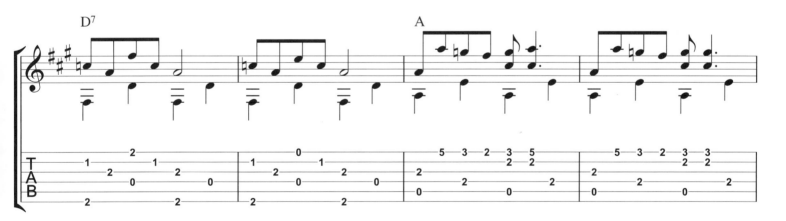

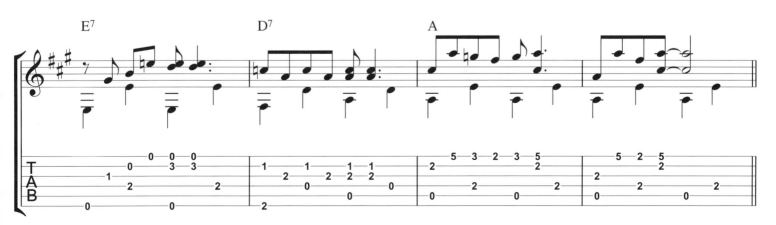

THE COMPLETE ACOUSTIC BLUES GUITAR METHOD

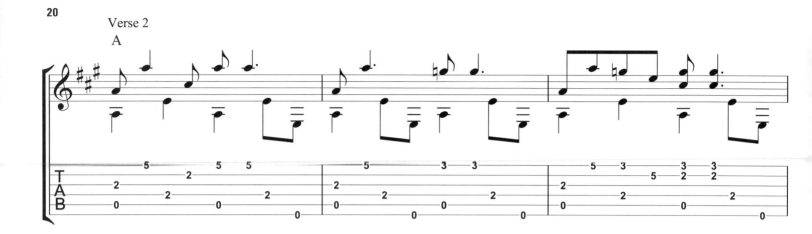
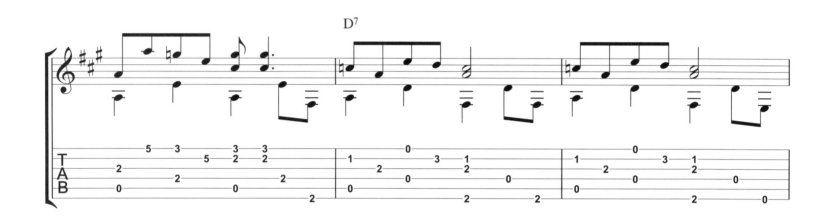
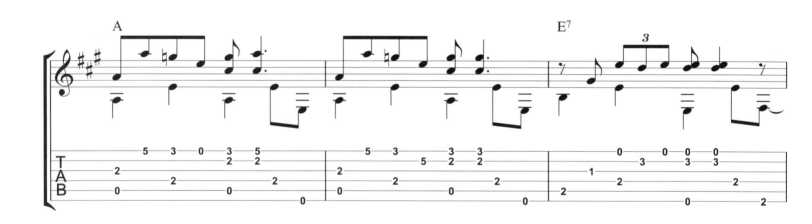
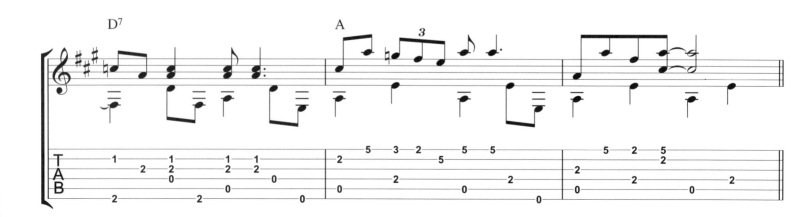

Verse 3

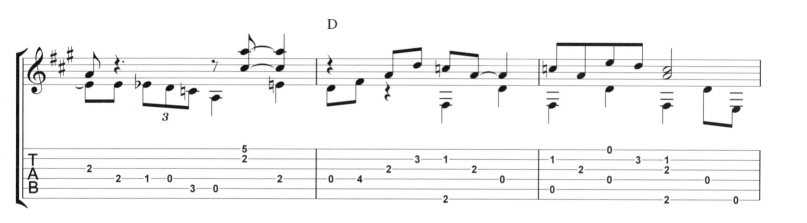
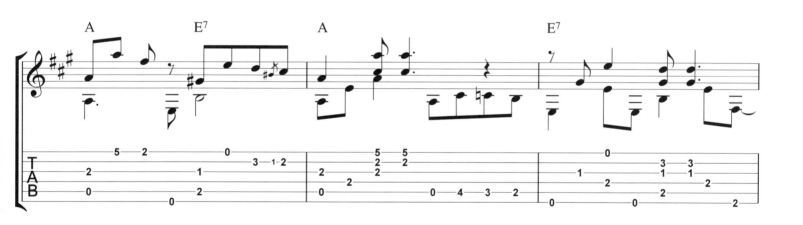
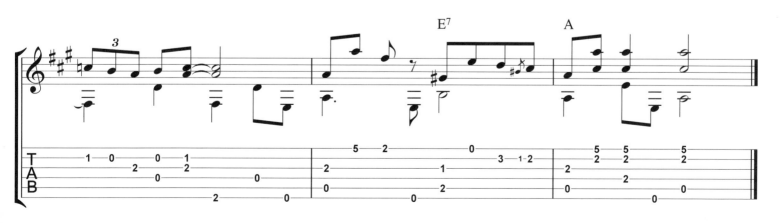

THE COMPLETE ACOUSTIC BLUES GUITAR METHOD

RICHARD'S RIFF

Richard "Hacksaw" Harney

Richard "Hacksaw" Harney was born in Money, Mississippi, in 1902. His recording career stretched more than a half-century, from the 1920s to the 1970s. His style is quite varied and can remind listeners of hard-core Delta blues players like Robert Johnson while at other times can echo the ragtime flair of Blind Blake or Willie McTell. Harney's last recording, "Sweet Man," on Adelphi Records, was recorded in 1970, and gives listeners a rare chance to hear a blues veteran recorded on state-of-the-art equipment. Harney died on Christmas Day, 1973.

The last piece, "Richard's Riff" illustrates more rhythmic syncopation in both bass and melody, a faster chord movement, and double-stop (two-note) riffs played out of the main chord positions. There is no pattern in the picking, only the changing rhythms of each phrase. This is based on a tune I learned from the great blues guitarist Richard "Hacksaw" Harney, who initially recorded in the 1920s as part of the duo Pet and Can. He continued to play in his later years, recording and performing in the early 70s.

 Standard tuning

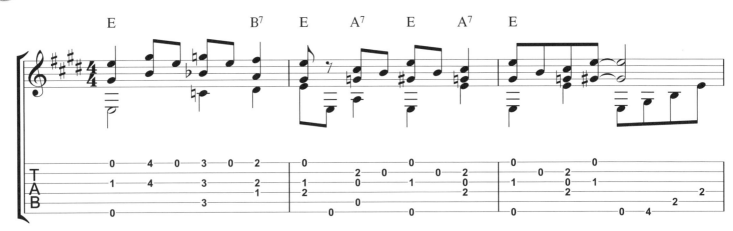

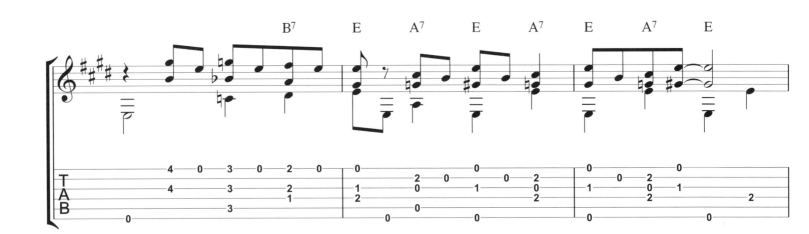

Once you gain a greater independence of the bass and melody lines, it becomes easier and more natural to create melodic and rhythmic variations. One of the main ingredients of blues playing is the ability to improvise within a tune, to create variations. Understanding what you are playing makes this easier. The best advice I can offer is to play slow—very slow—so that you can really feel the music. Then play a tune without the written music. In many of the pieces, I included additional sections with variations to give you some ideas for your own additional verses.

THE MUSIC

I have organized the tunes into a few very broad categories: **Fingerstyle Blues Basics**, **Ragtime Syncopation**, **Country Blues Styles**, **Open and Altered Tunings**, and **Expanding the Traditions**. In each listing, there is a suggested order of difficulty as well as the key and tuning that the song is played in.

- The pieces included in **Fingerstyle Blues Basics** illustrate some of the basic concepts of the picking techniques and chord ideas—for example, a quarter-note steady bass with a simple melody played off the chord shapes. Here would be a good place to begin.

- The **Ragtime Syncopation** section contains examples of tunes with more rhythmic syncopations in the bass and melody parts. These songs also have a faster chord movement and a more intricate melody. Once you feel comfortable with the steady bass idea of the tunes in the blues basics section, these would be a good next step.

- **Country Blues Styles** covers a wide variety of arrangements and techniques based on the playing styles or recordings of some of the most popular— as well as obscure—blues artists, including Scrapper Blackwell, Robert Johnson, Blind Lemon Jefferson, Memphis Minnie, Big Bill Broonzy, Reverend Gary Davis, Lonnie Johnson, Otis Harris and others. The techniques include double thumbing, damping, brushing, partial chords, and various rhythmic syncopations.

- Although the **Open and Altered Tunings** pieces represent many styles and could have been included under the classic styles above, I grouped them as a separate listing so you can get right to them. The arrangements are played in many of the most common (and not so common) open and altered tunings, including open D, open G, Drop D, open D minor, and drop DG. Highlighting some of the most popular themes of blues songs, these selections include chord positions in each tuning as well as a variety of picking techniques, syncopations, and melodic ideas.

- **Expanding the Traditions** is a collection of instrumentals based on the playing ideas of songs in the previous listings. At the same time, these songs also aim to create more contemporary sounding fingerstyle arrangements. I included an original classic ragtime arrangement, a few blues pieces with expanded forms and chord progressions, as well as a two gospel arrangements that use chord blocks to harmonize a melody line (a chord-melody approach). The gospel instrumentals are based on the playing of Rev. Gary Davis, one of the few artists—or perhaps the only artist—who used this idea as part of his gospel music guitar style.

Country blues traditions developed from the collective work of individual musicians. There are many ingredients that make up the music of a particular blues artist—most of which we may never know. It becomes an easy trap to broadly group the musicians and assign them a certain technique, style, or a regional territory such as Mississippi blues, Texas blues, Alabama, Piedmont, etc. For example, when you listen to the music of Charlie Patton, Mississippi John Hurt, Bo Carter, Skip James, and Robert Johnson—all from the Mississippi Delta—it is apparent how different their sound and playing style is. Even though there seems to be a dominant song, guitar key, or melodic idea that was adopted in a certain region, categorizing blues can miss the mark. The main lesson is that the beauty of the music is in the individual artist.

FINGERSTYLE BLUES BASICS

KEY	
C	Creole Baby
G	Bye Bye Blues
C	John C's Rag
D	Good Feeling Blues
C	Ragtime Strut
G	Barrelhouse Blues

RAGTIME SYNCOPATION

KEY	
C	Durham Dance
C	Come On Boys
C	Black Cat Blues
C	Ragging the Blues
G	Do I Have to Wait?
C	East Coast Rag
G	Do Anything If You Let Me

COUNTRY BLUES STYLES

KEY	
A	Blues in A
E	Lonesome Man Blues
E	Lordy Lord Blues
A	The Devil and Me
E	Baby Come Back
E	Little Vicksburg
A	Old Time Blues
A	Texas Nights
E	Richard's Riff
A	Mistreating Woman
A	Texarkana Valley
E	Highway Bound
E	River Blues
E	Papa Charlie's Blues
C	The Dirt Road
E	Bo's Blues
A	Mr. Jefferson's Blues

OPEN AND ALTERED TUNINGS

KEY	
Drop D	Beale Street Rock
Open D	Tampa Blues
Open G	What's the Matter?
Open D	Good Girl
Drop D	Big Road
Open G	Fandango in Open G
Open D Minor	Skippy's Blues
Open G	Mississippi Moan
Drop GD	You Got to Know How
Open G	Blues Ain't Gone
Drop DG	Blues in G
Open D	Police Blues
Drop D	Jump Blues
Drop D	Farewell Baby

EXPANDING THE TRADITIONS

KEY	
G	Sunday Church Meeting
E	Hudson River Boogie
A	Sunset Lake Rag
G	Spiritual for R.G.D.
G	Virginia Stomp
Open D	At Midnight
E	Delta Nights

THE COMPLETE ACOUSTIC BLUES GUITAR METHOD

FINGERSTYLE BLUES BASICS

JOHN C'S RAG

"John C's Rag" is based on an alternating bass (on the beat) picking style. In the first part, the simple melody is played on top. Part two has the same picking approach with a more complicated chord progression that uses partial or two notes positions of the chord. The melody is constantly weaving throughout the positions. This is good instrumental to learn for developing a solid picking technique. I wrote this for the great "Piedmont blues" champion and good friend John Cephas.

 Standard tuning

Part 1

Swing (♫ = ♩♪)

GOOD FEELING BLUES

This is a beautiful and melodic blues in the key of D. In the first four bars, the melody riffs are played out of the chord positions with a steady alternating bass. Try to keep the full chord positions held down while playing the riffs. This song is based on a Blind Blake's recording "Bad Feeling Blues." It is one of his most unusual songs and one of the few he played in the key of D.

Drop D tuning:
D A D G B E

Swing ($\sqrt{}\sqrt{} = \sqrt{}^{3}\sqrt{}$)

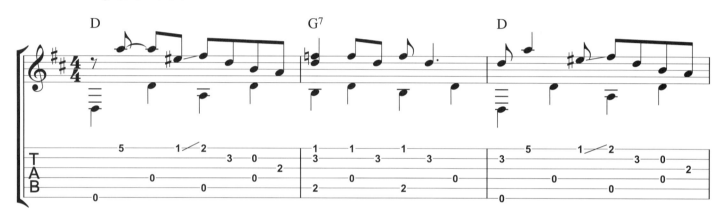

RAGTIME STRUT

Blind Boy Fuller

Piedmont blues guitarist Blind Boy Fuller was born as Fulton Allen in 1907, in Wadesboro, North Carolina. By the time Fuller turned twenty-one, he had completely lost his eyesight and he earned his living from entertaining at house parties, in the tobacco warehouses and on street corners in the Winston-Salem and Durham areas. By the late 1930s, Fuller had been discovered and he recorded more than 120 sides for various labels. The influence of guitar masters Blind Blake and Rev.

This is a 32-bar ragtime piece in two parts using a classic ragtime chord progression. In the first part the chords are C, A7, D7, G7, and in the middle section, C, C7, F, A♭7. There's a classic bass and melody line moving from the D7 to G chord. This is another good one to start with as it has an alternating bass throughout.

Gary Davis are apparent in Fuller's styling. Davis indicated that Fuller had learned guitar from him and noted, "He would have been alright if I kept him under me long enough." Fuller died of natural causes in Durham, North Carolina in 1941.

RAGTIME SYNCOPATION

DURHAM DANCE

Many ragtime blues tunes are based on the rhythms of local dances. "Durham Dance" is based on riffs I learned from Rev. Gary Davis, who played an assortment of "Buck Dances," "Fox Trots," and "Two Steps," as well as novelty songs, such as "Sally Where'd You Get Your Liquor From," that have a dance-like groove. Both parts of the tune feature chromatic riffs using double stops (two strings played at the same time), played as eight-note riffs moving through the progression. The chords are fairly simple, although the way these riffs move in and out of the basic chords can be tricky.

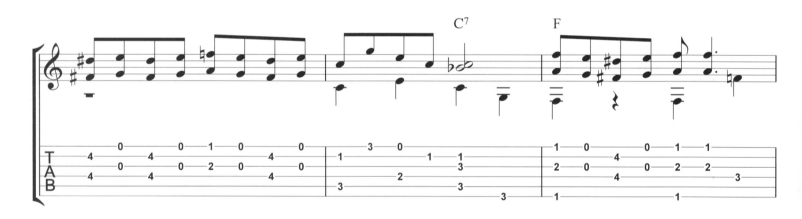

COME ON BOYS

"Come On Boys" is based on the ragtime playing of Blind Blake. Loosely based on his recording of "Come On Boys, Let's Do That Messing Around," the arrangement features his trademark picking style: a highly syncopated bass played under the melodic riffs. The thumb is doing all the work, "dragging" from string to string with each stroke to create a full strum-like sound.

Standard tuning

Bouncy ($\sqrt{} = \sqrt[3]{}\sqrt{}$)

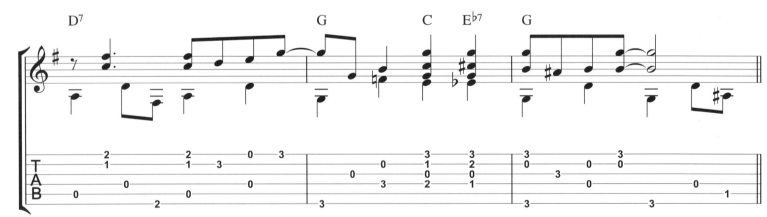

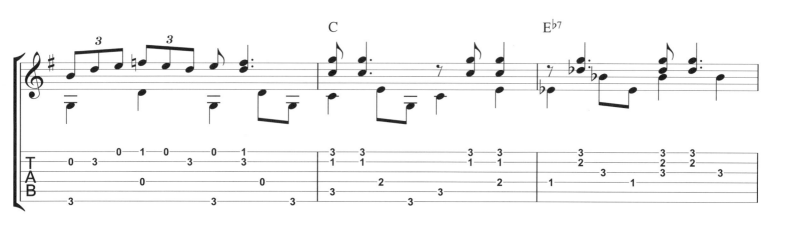
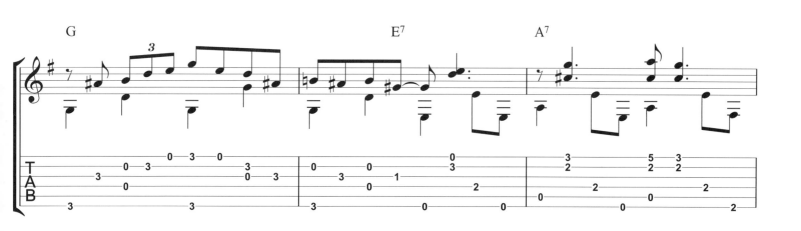
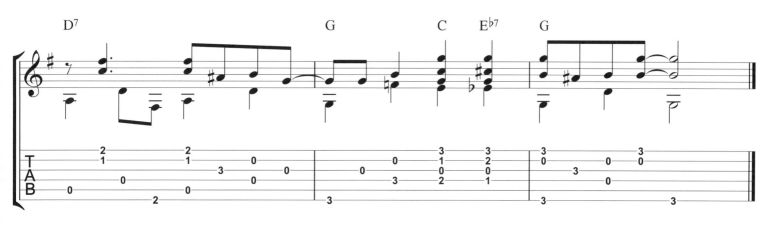

BLACK CAT BLUES

"Black Cat Blues" is a 12-bar ragtime blues song inspired by Blind Blake's recordings of "Black Dog Blues" and "Early Morning Blues." It illustrates his classic style of syncopated picking and many of his trademark riffs in the key of C. The bass is constantly shifting on and off the beat, creating his unique bounce and groove. Blake was constantly improvising his way through a tune. Try listening to his recordings for further ideas and variations.

Standard tuning

Swing (♪♪ = ♪³♪)

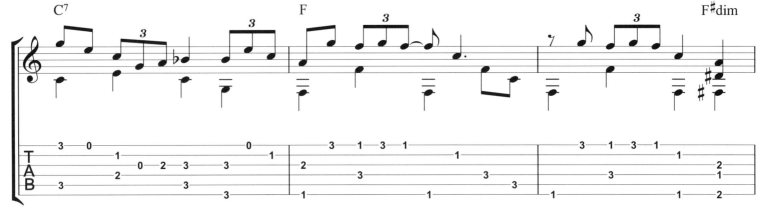

RAGGING THE BLUES

"Ragging the Blues" is an 8-bar blues instrumental with a ragtime feel. It is based on a melody I learned from Rev. Davis. It is typical of the melodic and syncopated approach of his guitar playing. In measures 5 through 8, the cadence moves through a series of small chord shapes and the ending in the second verse is extended with a classic turnaround played by barring the top four strings on the 5th fret and moving the second and fourth strings in contrary motion. This is a good one for further variations.

Standard tuning

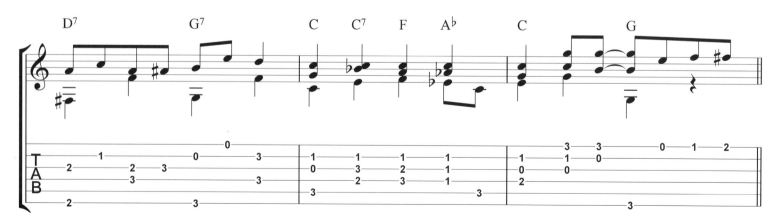

DO I HAVE TO WAIT?

This is a classic 12-bar ragtime blues melody showcasing a variety of Rev. Gary Davis's trademark riffs, chord shapes and swing. It is a version of his recordings of "Hesitation Blues," of which each performance was a different improvisation. I wrote out two verses with variations in the melody and bass. The intricate lines of the first and second endings can be a little tricky to play. Here, the bass part on the sixth and fourth strings should be played with the thumb.

Standard tuning

Swing (♪♪ = ♪♩)

EAST COAST RAG

Blind Blake

Although renowned as one of the most skilled guitarists of his generation, Blake remains a historically obscure, enigmatic figure. He hailed from Jacksonville, Florida, and spent some time in Chicago. His debut record, "West Coast Blues," recorded in Chicago in 1926, was the only commercially successful guitar instrumental of the era. In 1932, he recorded about eighty songs. After his record company went bankrupt in 1932, he moved (disappeared) from Chicago. It is unclear where and when he died. Little else is known about him.

"East Coast Rag" is perhaps the most difficult ragtime instrumental in this collection. It is based on Blind Blake's classic recordings of "West Coast Blues" and "Southern Rag," two of his greatest instrumentals. It illustrates the way he would interweave the bass and melody lines to create his classic syncopated ragtime sound. In the first few measures, the heavy syncopation in the bass provides the momentum, while in part two, the bass starts out as an alternating pattern and the melody has all the rhythm. Blake was one of the most exciting blues and ragtime guitarists of his generation. His playing represents some of the most highly sophisticated guitar work in country blues. This one is tricky.

Standard tuning

Swing ($\sqrt{}\sqrt{} = \sqrt{}^{3}\sqrt{}$)

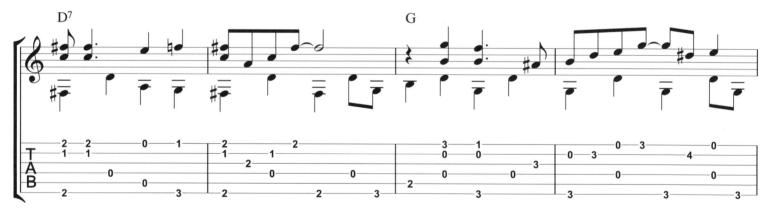

DO ANYTHING IF YOU LET ME

Reverend Gary Davis

Born in 1896 in Larens, South Carolina, Davis took up banjo and guitar as a child. Although his dedication to developing instrumental expertise did not hold a great interest for his original Southern audience, it brought him singular prestige in the 1960s and attracted numerous guitar students. His talent for voice leading and syncopation most likely was influenced by his time spent leading church congregations as a Baptist minister. Davis was still teaching and performing at the time of his death in New York in 1972.

I learned many versions of this piece from Rev. Davis. It is based on "Baby Let Me Lay It On You," a melody played by blues artists that also became popular with contemporary folk musicians. There is no set pattern to the picking, as each phrase has a different syncopation in the bass, with a moving melody throughout the progression. The E♭ chord is played in the C shape on the 6th fret.

Standard tuning

Medium Ragtime Bounce

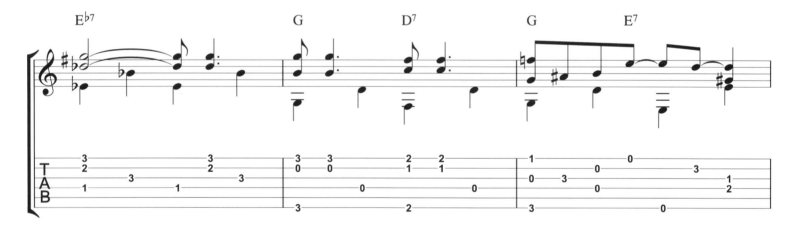

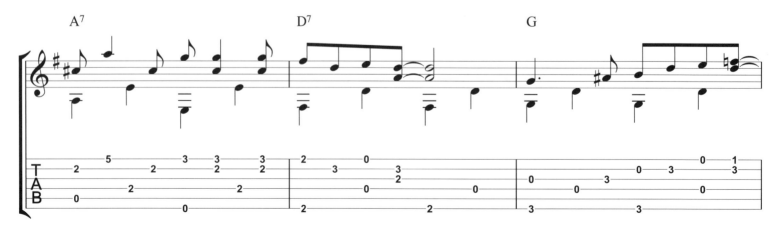

COUNTRY BLUES STYLES

LONESOME MAN BLUES

"Lonesome Man Blues" is an 18-bar blues in E. There is no picking pattern in the bass. It is sometimes steady (as in the first E phrase), before shifting around to a half-time feel in the second part. The descending bass riff in measures 13 through 15 moves through the E phrase. It is loosely based on the playing of Arthur Pettis and George Torey, two great obscure blues guitarists.

Standard tuning

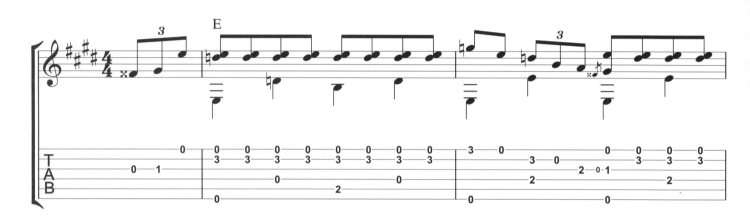

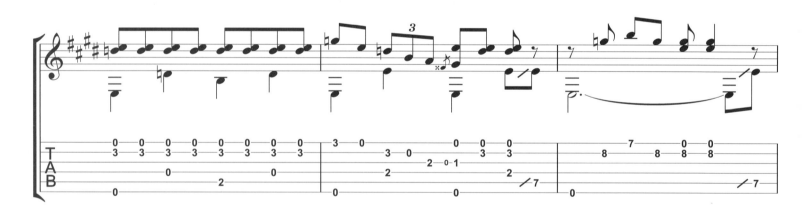

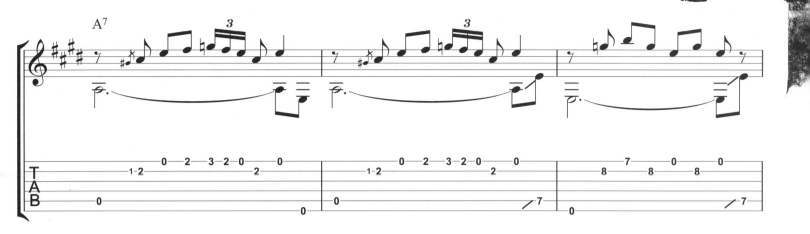
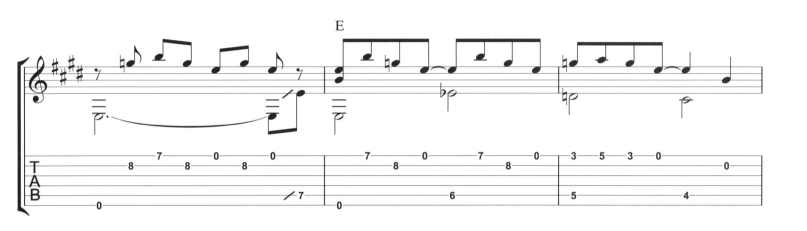
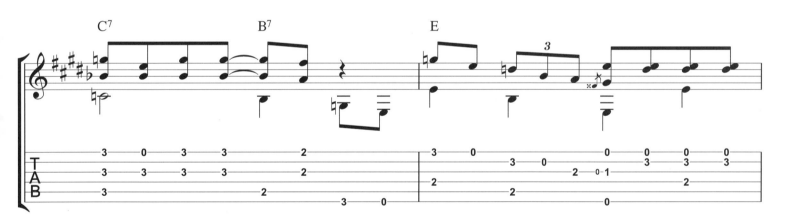
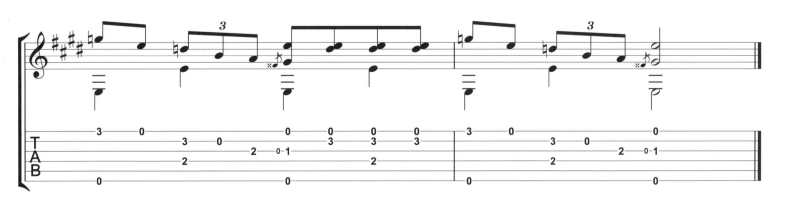

THE COMPLETE ACOUSTIC BLUES GUITAR METHOD

LORDY LORD BLUES

Teddy Darby

Theodore Roosevelt "Blind Teddy" Darby was born in 1902 in Henderson, Kentucky, and spent some of his younger years in a reformatory and in the municipal workhouse. After moving to St. Louis, Missouri, in the early 1920s, Darby teamed up with Petey Wheatstraw and Darby's cousin Tom Webb. Darby's recording career spanned eight years, from 1929 through 1937, when he recorded twenty-four titles under a variety of names for Bluebird, Paramount, Vocalion, and Victor. Darby gave up music entirely and became an ordained minister after Webb was murdered. He died sometime in the 1960s.

Many blues musicians played a version of this melody, including the famous "Rolling and Tumbling" blues version played by Hambone Willie Newbern and Robert Johnson. In this arrangement, there is no pattern in the picking. The vocal melody line, played against a drone high E string, trades phrases with the bass riff in a sort of question-and-answer—type movement. The dissonances and lack of chord changes give the tune a beautiful modal quality. I based this version on a recording by Blind Teddy Darby.

 Standard tuning

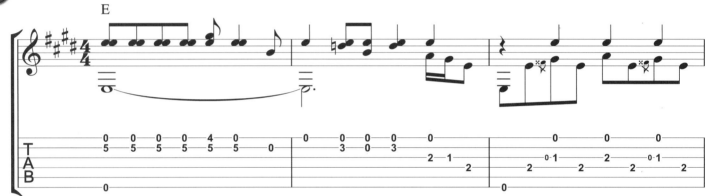

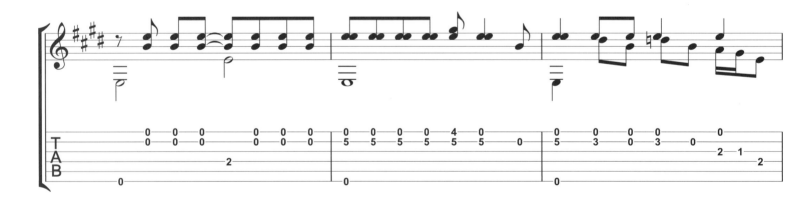

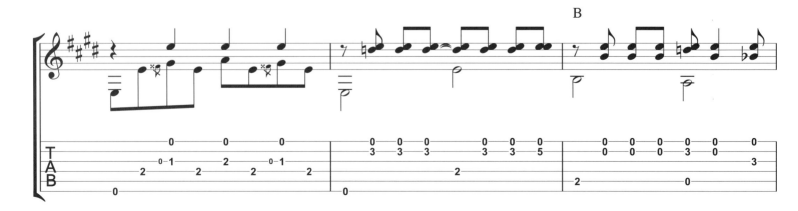

THE DEVIL AND ME

Robert Johnson

The most storied and copied figure in blues history, Johnson was born in 1912 and reared in the Delta town of Commerce, Tennessee, just below Memphis. He took up guitar in the late 1920s, learning from such musicians as Son House. In 1938, he was fatally poisoned while playing near Greenwood, Mississippi.

"The Devil and Me" is a blues inspired by the playing of Robert Johnson's recording of "Kindhearted Woman Blues" and "Me and the Devil." To capture the shuffle feel of the tune, I wrote it out in 12/8. The overall rhythmic feel is a slow triplet pulse where each beat is subdivided into three equal parts. The tricky (and beautiful) part of capturing the sound is the damping of the bass while at the same time letting the melody notes ring. The dynamics of each line are also different. This approach is like playing with two separate hands—no pattern picking.

 Standard tuning

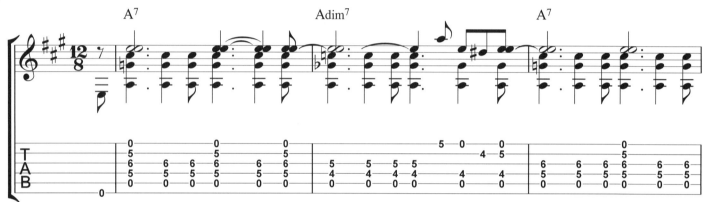

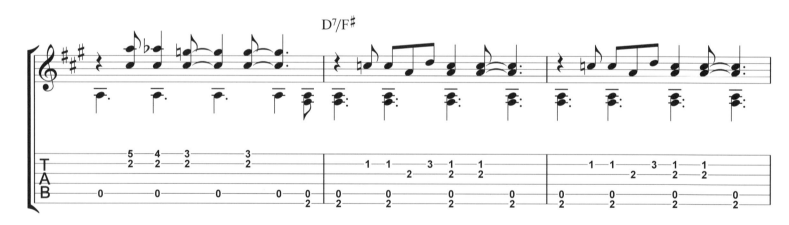

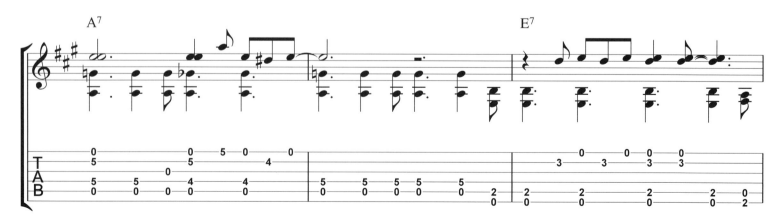

BABY COME BACK

"Baby Come Back" is a 12-bar blues in the key of E using a triplet idea (three equal notes to the beat) throughout the fast-moving melody line. The phrasing is another type of call-and-response approach where the melody states a riff and then the bass responds with an "answer" phrase, similar to "Lordy Lord Blues." The chords are all played as double stops (two strings), using open strings or partial positions to state the chord. The A chord riffs move very quickly in and out of the positions. There is definitely no pattern pick in this one.

 Standard tuning

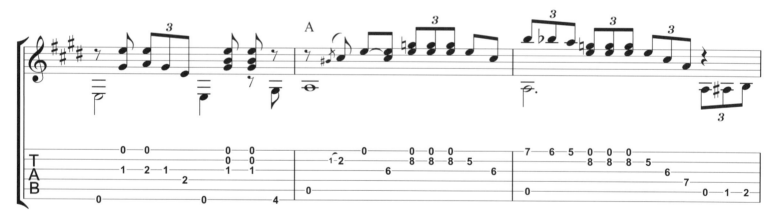

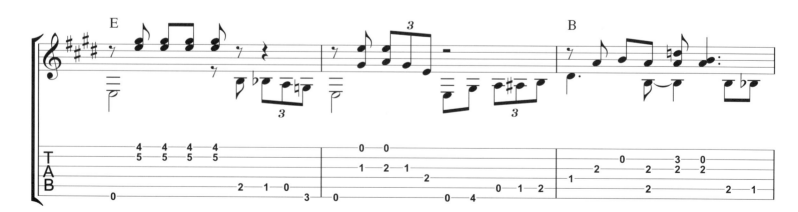

LITTLE VICKSBURG

Little Brother Montgomery

Eurreal Wilford "Little Brother" Montgomery was born near New Orleans in 1906. A gifted pianist at an early age, Montgomery was raised in the company of blues and jazz musicians in New Orleans including Jelly Roll Morton. After recording for Bluebird and Paramount in the 1920s and 1930s, Montgomery moved to Chicago in the early 1940s and established himself as a staple of the Chicago blues and jazz scene for the next thirty years. Among his notable protégés in Chicago were Otis Rush and Buddy Guy. He died in 1985 in Chicago.

"Little Vicksburg" is a version of the classic "Vicksburg Blues" recorded by the great blues pianist Little Brother Montgomery. There are basically two chords, E and B, which fill out the arrangement. The A chord is a passing chord. There are some difficult reaches in the moving bass line, as in measure 2, so playing at very slow tempo makes it easier to move in and out of these phrases. (The tune also sounds better that way.)

OLD TIME BLUES

Carl Martin

Carl Martin was born in 1906 in Stone Mountain, in the Appalachian region of Virginia. His musical career as a guitarist, mandolin player, and violin player spanned for than 50 years and his repertoire included blues, jug band, jazz, standards, and novelty tunes. Martin's earliest recordings were made in the mid-1930s and featured Piedmont and ragtime styles on tunes including "Crow Jane," "Old Time Blues," and a dozen other songs. Martin teamed up with Ted Bogan and Howard Armstrong and by the late 1930s their trio Martin, Bogan, and Armstrong was a staple in Chicago and the Midwest. Later in his career, Martin focused most of his musical skills on the mandolin. Carl Martin died in 1979.

"Old Time Blues" is based on the elegant and intricate playing of Carl Martin. The syncopations move quickly from the bass to the melody, as in the sixteenth-note phrases. The chord positions use partial shapes or just use two notes that cadence from phrase to phrase. Even though you are not holding down the full position, it's a good idea to "see" the shape the riff is based out of, as in the C7 and F#7 chords.

 Standard tuning

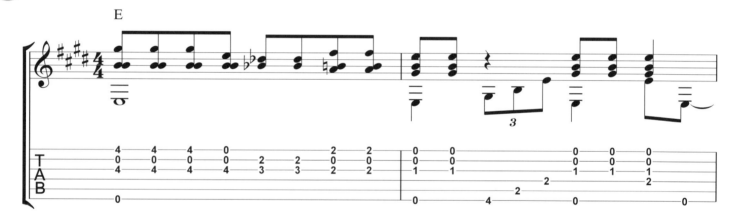

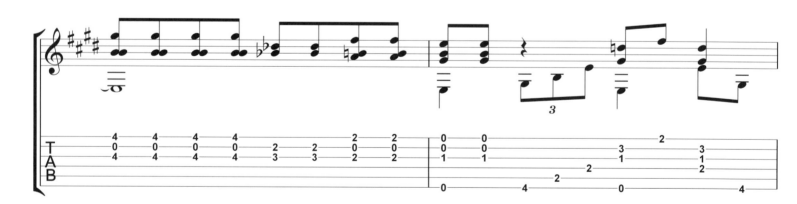

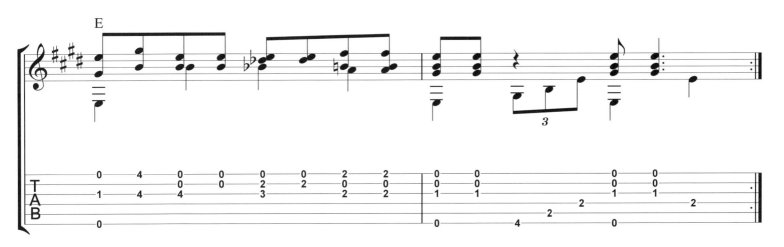

THE COMPLETE ACOUSTIC BLUES GUITAR METHOD

TEXAS NIGHTS

Here is a 12-bar blues in the key of A that features a steady rhythmic pulse using a driving bass line against the riffs in the melody. As in the playing of the Texas blues greats such as Funny Papa Smith, Blind Lemon Jefferson, Little Hat Jones, and Willie Reed, this tune is meant to be played with an accented bass feel. One way to do this "heavy" bass feel is to damp the bass part while keeping the melody ringing, a kind of half-damp where just the bass is damped by the palm of your hand.

Standard tuning

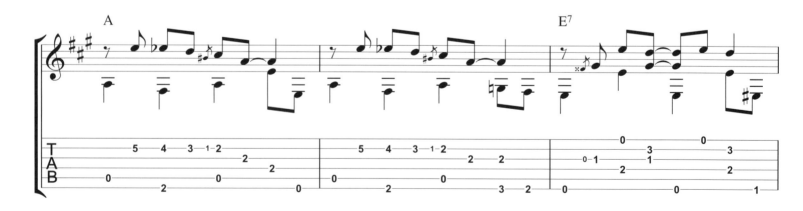

MISTREATING WOMAN

Blind Willie McTell

Born William Samuel McTier in either 1901 or 1898 in Thompson, Georgia, Blind Willie McTell began his recording career in 1927 for Victor Records. McTell was a master of ragtime, playing complex rhythms and dizzying melody lines on a twelve-string guitar. His repertoire was not limited to ragtime; McTell was also a master of gospel, blues, and even pop standards. McTell recorded under various aliases, for different recording labels, including Blind Sammie, Georgia Bill, Hot Shot Willie, Blind Willie, Red Hot Willie Glaze, Barrelhouse Sammie, and Pig & Whistle Red. He spent most of his life in and around Atlanta, Georgia. McTell died in 1959 in Milledgeville, Georgia.

"Mistreating Woman" is a tricky 16-bar blues that begins on the IV chord (D). The riffs played off the chords move quickly in and out of the positions, as in measure 4, where the melody shifts out of the position to the bass riffs. This one is meant to be played at a medium-to-fast tempo. The way to get the speed up is to play very slowly to get chord position movement smooth, and then get the feel of the syncopation while you play the riffs.

Standard tuning

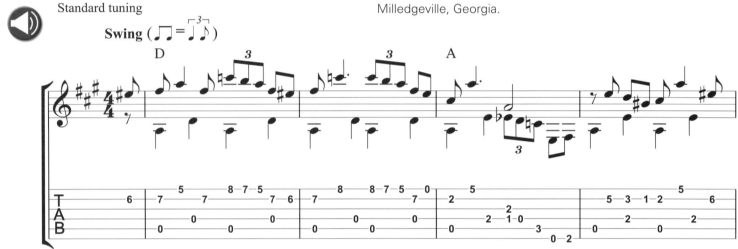

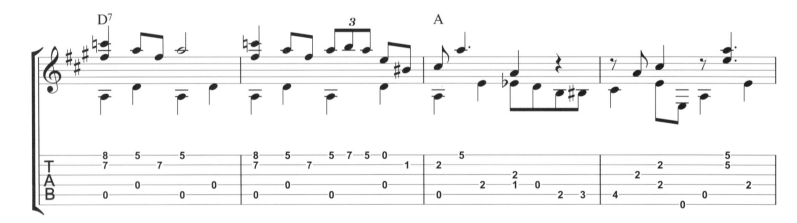

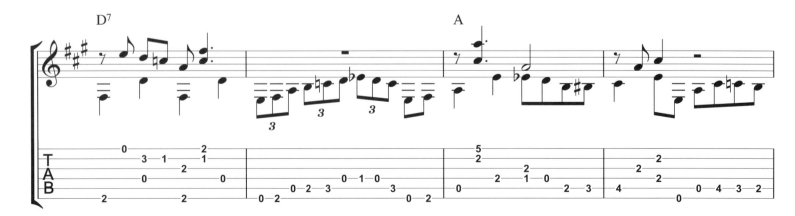

TEXARKANA VALLEY

"Texarkana Valley" is based on the playing of the obscure but no less great Texas blues artist Willie Reed. This 12-bar blues in the key of A is played with a steady monotonic (one note) bass with a few melodic riffs on top. The bass should be damped throughout, as a sort of "percussion" bass, to provide the steady driving rhythmic pulse. At the same time, the melody should be played lightly and ring out, similar to the idea in "Texas Nights Blues."

Standard tuning

Fast and steady

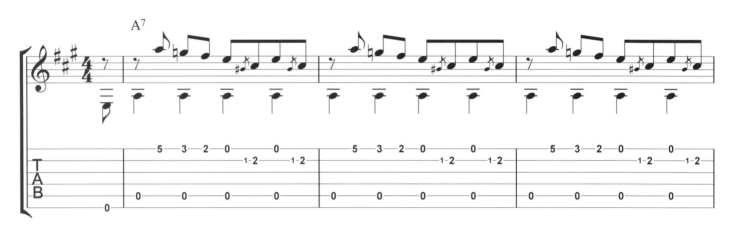

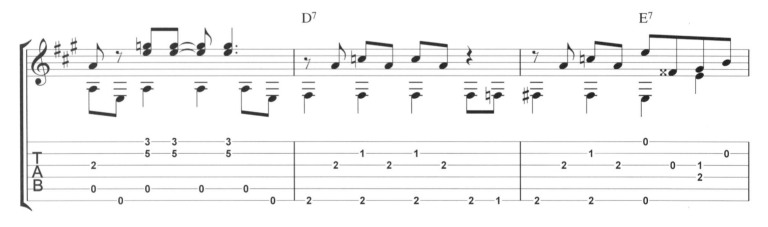

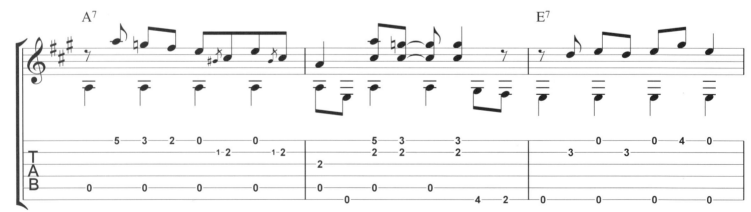

HIGHWAY BOUND

Big Bill Broonzy

Big Bill was born William Lee Conley Broonzy in Scott, Mississippi, in 1898, and reared as one of seventeen children in Pine Bluff, Arkansas. Broonzy's uncle taught him to play fiddle, and he began to perform local concerts. In 1920, he came to Chicago, and by 1927, he was recording for Paramount with various bands. Broonzy composed more than 350 pieces and achieved considerable popularity in both the Chicago blues scene as well as in Europe in the 1950s. He authored his autobiography *Big Bill Blues* in 1955 and died in 1958.

"Highway Bound" is a version of the classic 8-bar chord progression that was very popular with most blues guitarists: I / V / IV / IV / I / V / I / I. The sequence became known as the "Crow Jane" progression. "Highway Bound" is based on Big Bill Broonzy's popular "Key to the Highway." This arrangement begins with an E chord played as a first-position D chord moved up two frets.

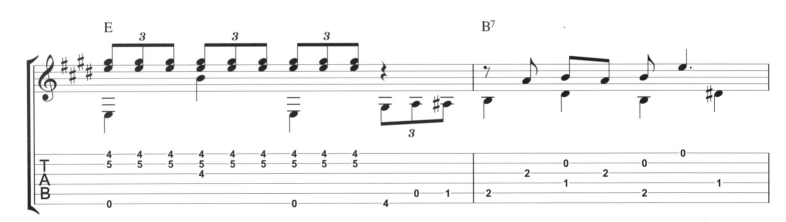

RIVER BLUES

Charlie Patton

Born in 1891, Charlie Patton was the Mississippi Delta's most popular blues entertainer for a quarter of a century. His tremendous baritone and facility with dance rhythms were first recorded in 1929 for the Paramount label. Between 1929 and 1930, Patton produced forty-two issued sides, more than any blues recording act had ever turned out in a single year. He died in 1934.

The strum-like sound of "River Blues" is played by brushing both the bass and melody parts. Even though the music is notated as one bass or melody string, brush across more than one string at a time to achieve a full, rich sound as you pick. This is a basic element in getting the sound of traditional blues guitar playing. One great example of the beautiful subtleties of this sound is Charlie Patton's recording of "Green River Blues."

Standard tuning

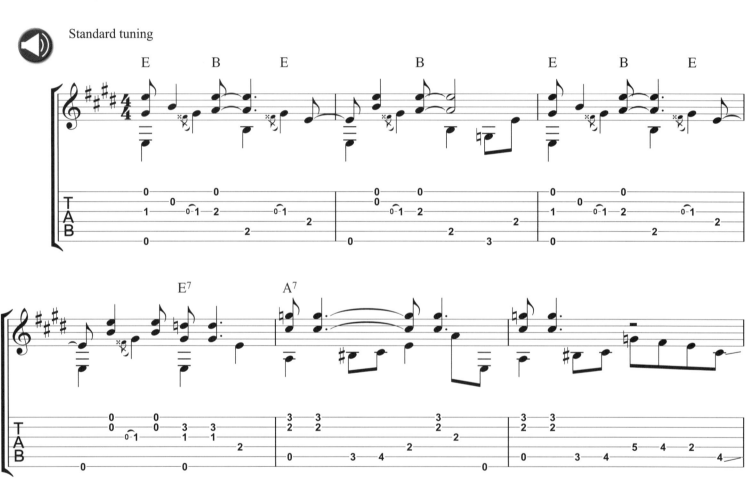

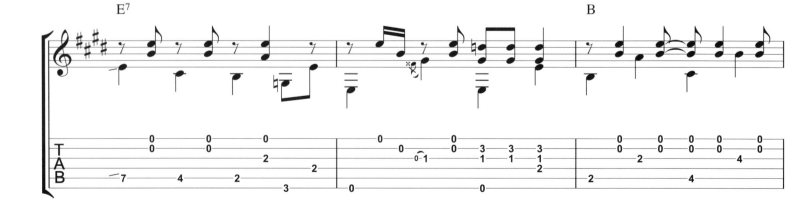

THE COMPLETE ACOUSTIC BLUES GUITAR METHOD

PAPA CHARLIE'S BLUES

Papa Charlie Jackson

Born in New Orleans in the mid-1880s, Charles "Papa Charlie" Jackson was a medicine show minstrel in Chicago, playing guitar, a hybrid six-string banjo, and ukulele. His recordings enjoyed commercial success and led him to record with Blind Blake, Big Bill Broonzy, Ma Rainey and Ida Cox. He recorded for Paramount and Okeh. His most famous songs include "Salty Dog Blues" and "Shake That Thing." He died in Chicago in 1938.

"Papa Charlie's Blues" is a ragtime blues played in the key of E, an unusual key for this type of tune. I based it on Papa Charlie Jackson's playing style and his recording of "Shave 'Em Dry." His fingerstyle technique is one of the most syncopated and complex in country blues. This song is an example that shows syncopated bass and melody lines moving through a ragtime chord progression. The bridge is based on Blind Lemon Jefferson's guitar break in his recording of "One Dime Blues." Play this one slow until you get the groove.

Standard tuning

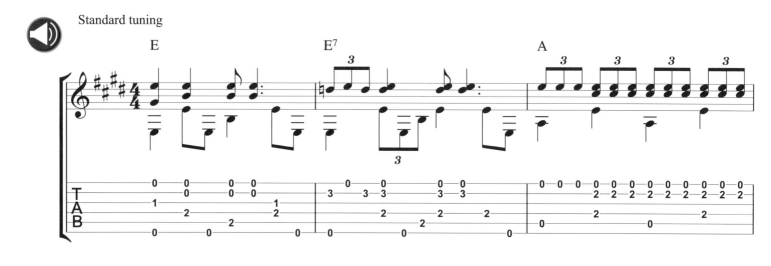

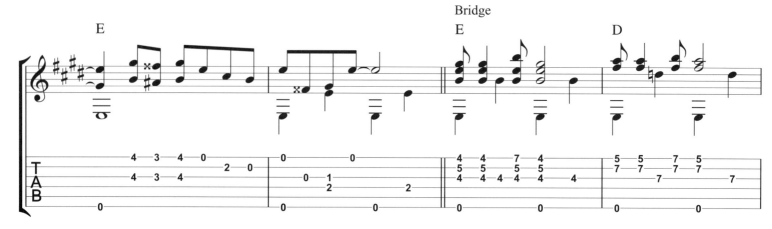

THE DIRT ROAD

"The Dirt Road" is a very unusual and tricky guitar arrangement. It's melodic and rhythmic approach uses challenging chord positions and highly rhythmic syncopations throughout each phrase. The melody and structure are also unique and very different from the previous styles.

The tune begins with a series of descending chord shapes from the 8th fret. This position is based out of a simple C chord shape but with the third string added to the position, making it a major 6th chord. The overall rhythmic feel is a slow half-time. The melodic riffs are subdivided into smaller rhythmic parts while the bass feel is simpler, with the emphasis on every few beats. I based this composition on the recording of "Down the Dirt Road" by Charlie Patton.

Standard tuning

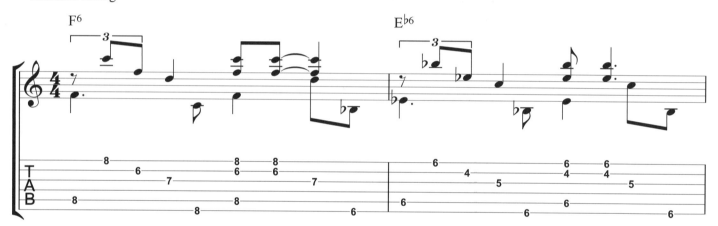

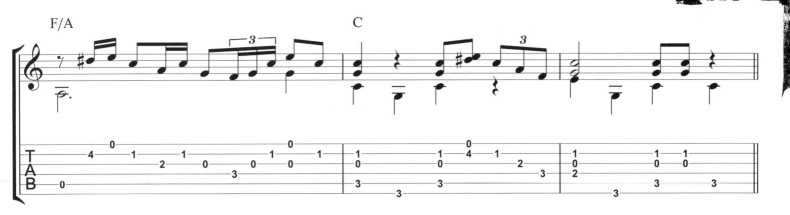

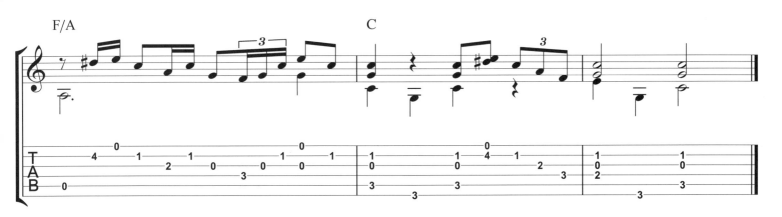

BO'S BLUES

Bo Carter

Armenter "Bo Carter" Chatmon was born in Bolton, Mississippi, in 1893. Carter became one of the best-known blues artists of his time, largely as a result of lively and sophisticated tunes packed with sexual innuendo. His career included several years as a member of the Mississippi Sheiks, a string band that included his brothers. His solo career includes more than 100 sides recorded in the 1930s. Carter died in 1964 in Memphis.

What gives this song its unique bounce is the rhythm and swing of the bass, which accents the second and fourth beats of each measure. Once you get the interplay between the lines, it becomes easier to play faster. Three chords—E, A, and B—are played in various and sometimes unusual positions on the fingerboard from the 1st to the 12th frets. "Bo's Blues" is inspired by the playing of Bo Carter.

Standard tuning

Swing (♪♪ = ♪♪³)

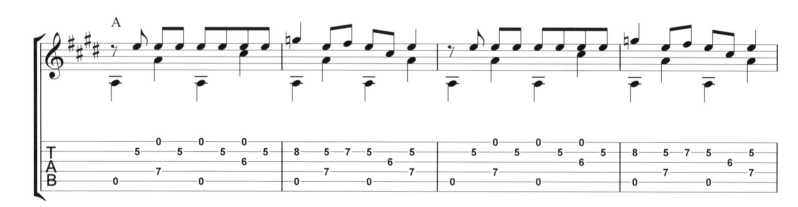

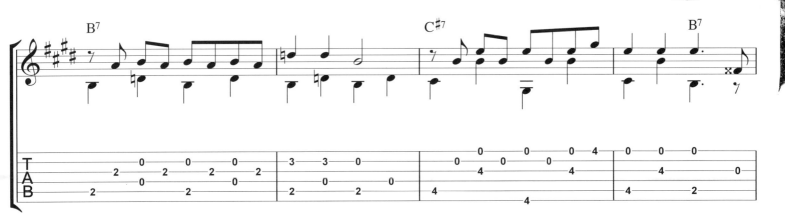

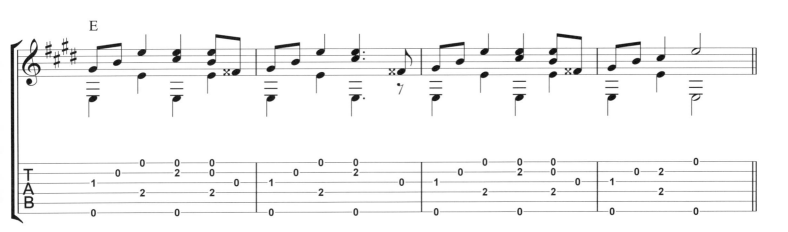

Verse 2

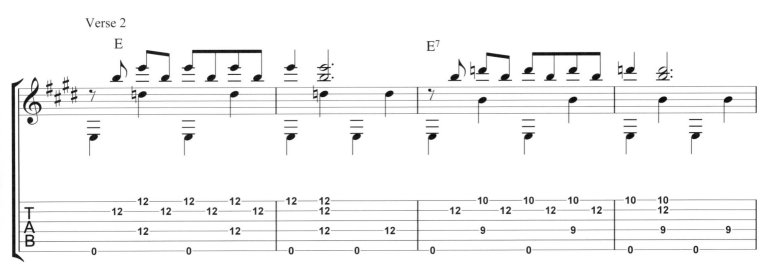

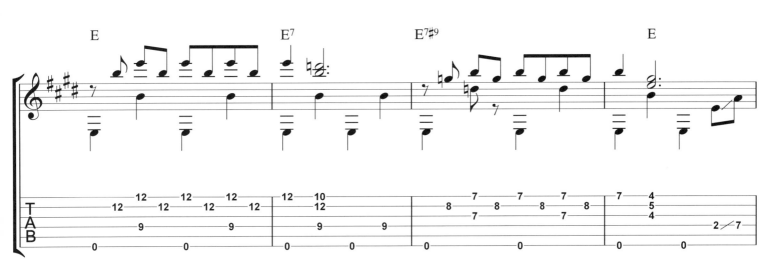

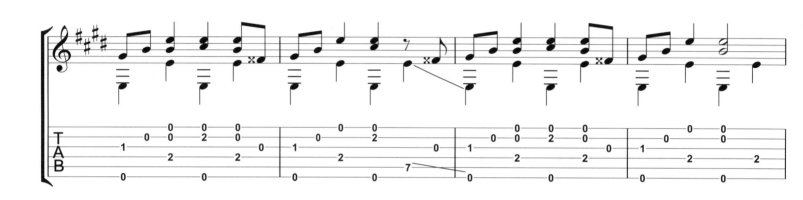
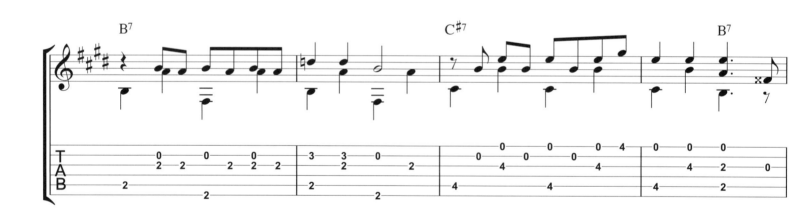

MR. JEFFERSON'S BLUES

Blind Lemon Jefferson was perhaps the most original blues artist of his time, as well as one of the most popular. His recordings represent some of the greatest (and most complicated) guitar work of his generation. In "Mr. Jefferson's Blues," I illustrated some of his signature ideas and techniques based on his famous recording of "Matchbox Blues," one of the true "hits" in country blues. This tune is played in the key of A.

Jefferson played fast.

One way to feel the subtleties and be able to play the riffs easier and with swing would be to play the song with a half-time feel. In other words, although the tune is written in a 4/4 time signature, try to feel each measure in two-beat pulses, or a slow 2/4 feel. This gives more rhythmic "room" to play the intricate rhythms of the melody. Playing against the half-note bass line—really feeling the space between the beats—is also one of the ways to open up the phrasing and play at faster tempos.

The melody-line riffs are all based around the smaller chord shapes. For example, the A chord measures are instead played in the D shape on the 9th fret. The bass line changes in measures 7 through 9, creating a more syncopated feel. The added bar at the end of each verse is played as a thumb strum.

Blind Lemon Jefferson

Lemon Jefferson was born in Wortham, Texas, in 1897. Blind from birth, Jefferson spent most of his early years as a street singer in eastern Texas. Jefferson was discovered by a talent scout for Paramount Records in 1926 and was brought to Chicago where he recorded 100 songs under the name "Blind Lemmon Jefferson," and a handful of spirituals under the name "Deacon Bob." Success came quickly to the blind bluesman; his recordings were at the forefront of the race records craze and earned him, among other things, an automobile from Paramount. Jefferson's recordings are distinguished by his high and eerie vocal styling coupled with a distinct and free guitar phrasing. Jefferson's life and career were short. He died of mysterious causes in Chicago in 1929. He was not driving at the time.

THE COMPLETE ACOUSTIC BLUES GUITAR METHOD

Standard tuning

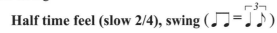

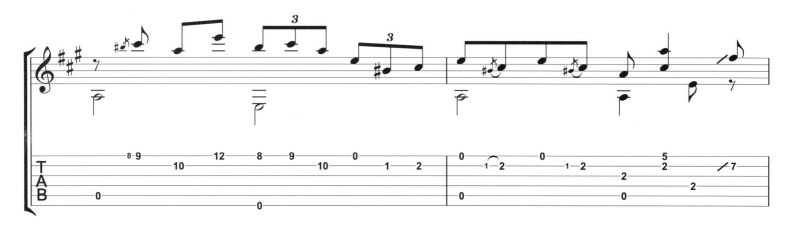

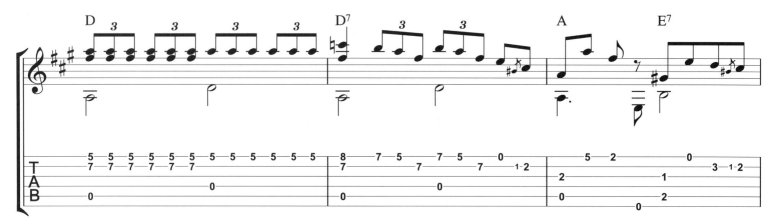

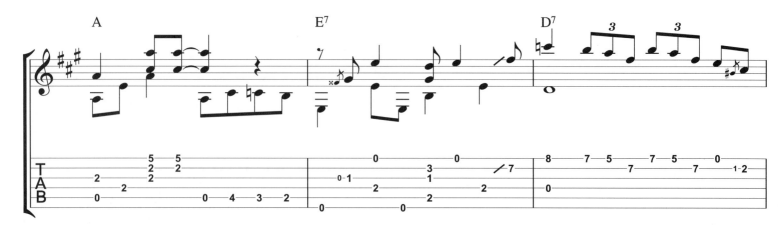

OPEN AND ALTERED TUNINGS

BEALE STREET ROCK

Willie Moore

Born in Dover, Georgia, he was the only Virginian country bluesman to record for the Paramount label. His few recorded sides include "Ragtime Millionaire," "Old Country Rock," and "One Way Gal." He died in Warrenton, Virginia, in 1955.

"Beale Street Rock" is good place to begin playing in Drop D tuning (D A D G B E). The alternating bass, simple riffs, and chord positions lay out the basics. Although it is in the key of D, it starts out on a G chord using only two fretted notes. The tune is another illustration of the basic alternating bass line approach, but has a syncopated variation in the E7 and A7 bars in the second ending. This is loosely based on the recording of "Old Country Rock" by Willie Moore.

Dropped D tuning:
D A D G B E

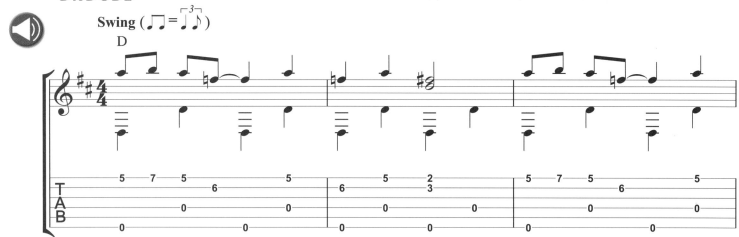

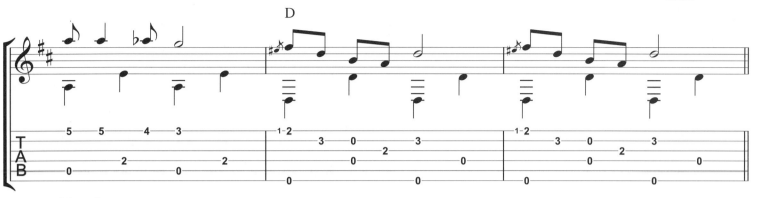

Verse 2

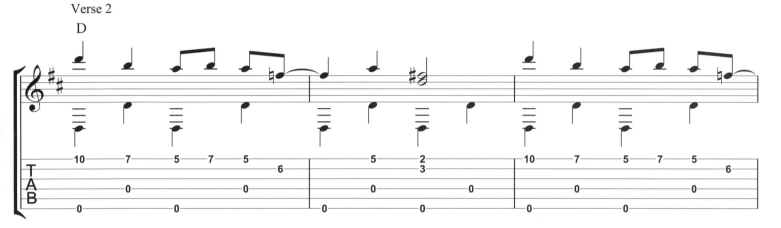

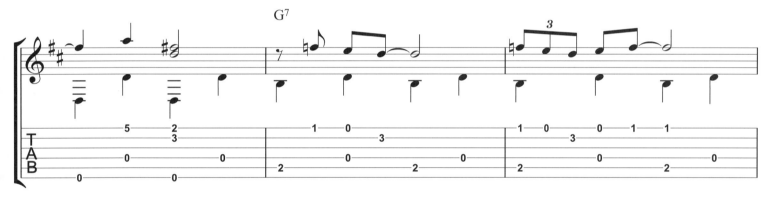

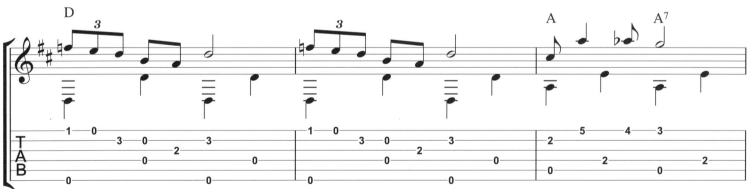

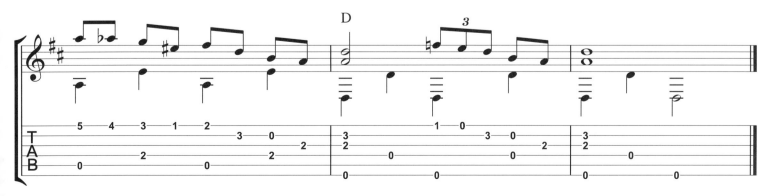

TAMPA BLUES

Tampa Red

Tampa Red, the "Guitar Wizard," was born in 1904 in Smithville, Georgia, and had a long and prolific recording career in Chicago. Primarily a slide player on a National Steel guitar, Tampa Red recorded in a variety of styles from vaudeville tunes to soulful blues. Among his collaborators during the 1930s and 1940s was pianist Georgia Tom Dorsey. Red died in Chicago in 1981.

This is a good tune to get comfortable playing in Open D tuning (D A D F# A D). It uses the main D, G, and A7 positions, as well as some of the signature riffs used in Open D. The bass line is steady and alternating with some simple melody riffs played on top. Try brushing the bass strings to get a fuller sound and a more rhythmic drive. For example, as you play the low sixth string, play the fifth and fourth strings as well, as one stroke. When playing the fourth-string bass, play (brush through) the third string. The goal is to sound as if you are almost strumming the guitar rather than picking it.
This tune is based on the playing of Tampa Red.

WHAT'S THE MATTER?

"What's The Matter?" is in Open G tuning (D G D G B D) and illustrates the basic chord positions therein. This is a good one to start with to get the feel of playing in Open G. The two verses have a steady bass with a melody constantly riffing through the positions. The interplay is tricky, so master it slowly before playing at a fast tempo. The tune is inspired by the playing of the great Memphis Minnie (see Memphis Minnie's bio under "Steady Bass").

Open G tuning:
D G D G B D

Swing (♪♪ = ♪♪)

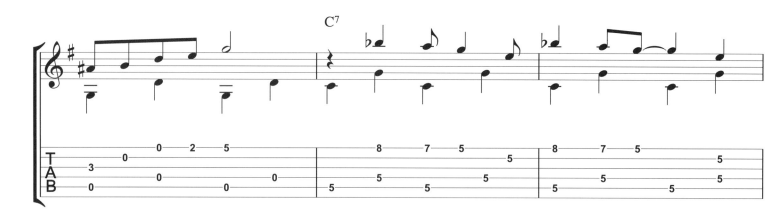

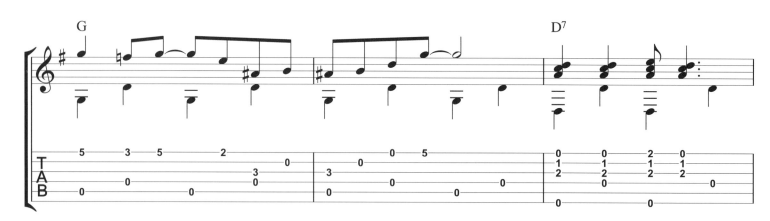

GOOD GIRL

"Good Girl" is based on a song I learned from the Josh White recording "Good Gal." Played in Open D tuning (D A D F♯ A D), it has the classic feel of ragtime blues with the added technique of snapping the bass strings. The idea is to bounce off the bass strings quickly, from one to the other. For instance, in the first four measures, play the quarter notes as eighth notes with an eighth rest, and the eighth-note bass notes as sixteenth notes with a sixteenth rest. Also, pull the string away from the guitar as you pluck the note—as in "snapping" the string. There are some tricky passages where the bass and melody crisscross so that your fingers play below your thumb.

Open D tuning:
D A D F♯ A D

Swing ($\sqrt{} = \sqrt[3]{}\sqrt{}$)

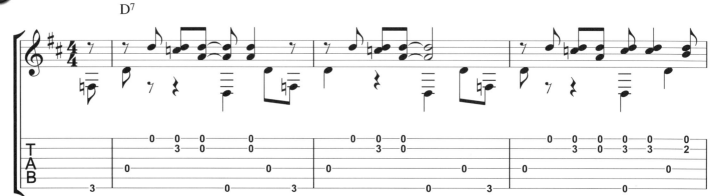

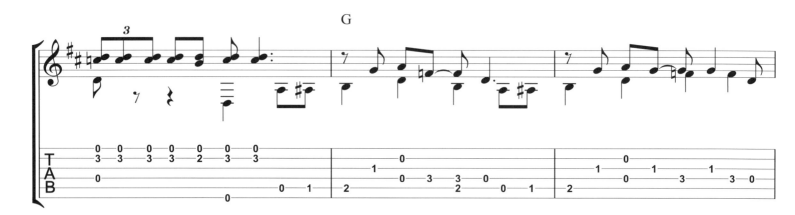

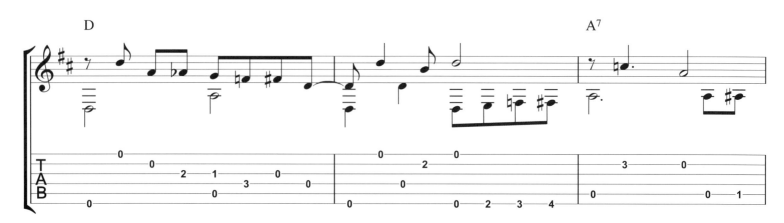

BIG ROAD

Tommy Johnson

Born in 1896 and reared in Terry, Mississippi, a town below Jackson, Tommy Johnson became a musician around 1914 after running away from home and spending two years in the Delta. During the 1920s, Johnson was the most popular bluesman in Jackson. His signature songs were local standards. He was still performing at the time of his death in 1956.

"Big Road," played in Drop D tuning (D A D G B E), is a version of a popular arrangement that many blues musicians recorded.

The arrangement has a very specific interplay between the bass and melody lines. The first four bars are played in the bass with melody only played on the upbeat. The next two bars are reversed, where the melody is played with only one bass note per bar. In these bars, play the melody by brushing your fingers across two strings as an upstroke to get the sound. In bars 7 and 8, the rhythms between the melody and bass parts can be tricky.

"Big Road" is based on Tommy Johnson's recording of "Big Road Blues."

 Drop D tuning:
D A D G B E

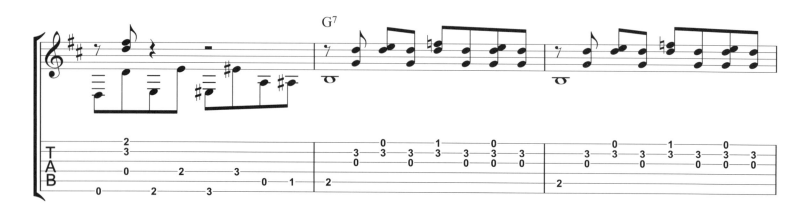

FANDANGO IN OPEN G

There were many recordings of "Spanish Fandango," a popular melody and one of the first written guitar instrumentals in Open G tuning, also called "Spanish" tuning (D G D G B D). The rhythm of this arrangement is, as always, in the bass. In this case, it is the dotted-quarter/eighth-note figure that provides the tango-like rhythm. The first sixteen bars have the melody stated on top, resolving differently in the first and second endings. In the variation section, I wrote out some further ideas on embellishing the melody.

Open G tuning:
D G D G B D

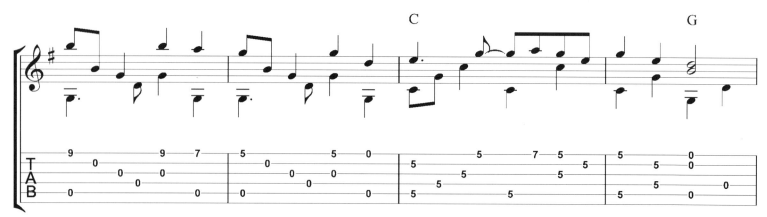

SKIPPY'S BLUES

Skip James

Born Nehemiah James in 1902, he was reared in Bentonia, Mississippi, a hill country town south of the Mississippi Delta. James was the only bluesman of his period to excel on both guitar and piano. Many of his original compositions feature guitar pieces in Open D Minor tuning which, along with his falsetto vocals, set James's music apart from his Mississippi counterparts. He died in 1969 while living in Philadelphia.

"Skippy's Blues" is based on the playing of the Mississippi guitarist Skip James, one of the few artists who played in Open D Minor tuning (D A D F A D). This 12-bar blues uses only two chords: D (or D7) and A7. Not using the G chord gives it even more of a minor tonality. In the first two bars, the melody is played on the fourth string. In the next two bars, there is the basic riff that appears throughout the song. The A7 is played by fretting the second and third strings on the 2nd fret. This is a great tune to experiment with the use of open strings to create new chord sounds and different textures in the picking, such as brushing, damping, and double-thumbing. "Skippy's Blues" uses some of these ideas. Skip James's recordings of "Devil Got My Woman" or "Hard Time Killing Floor" (both in Open D Minor) have some of the most beautiful and haunting sounds in blues music.

 Open D minor tuning:
D A D F A D

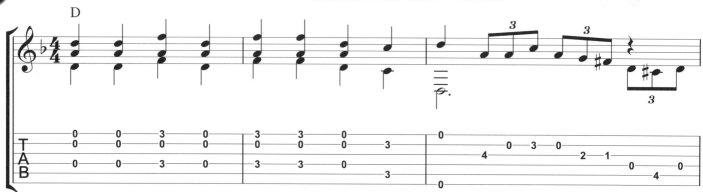

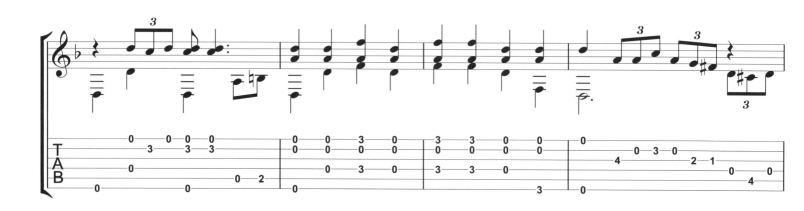

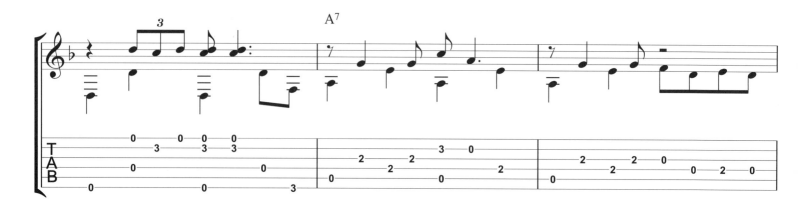

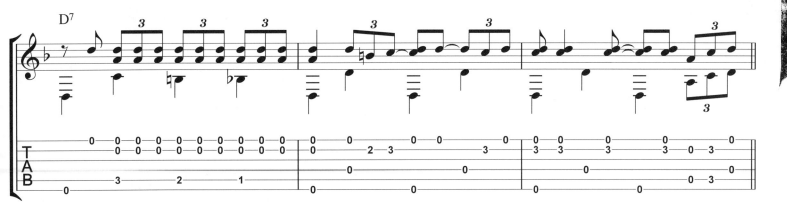

Verse 2

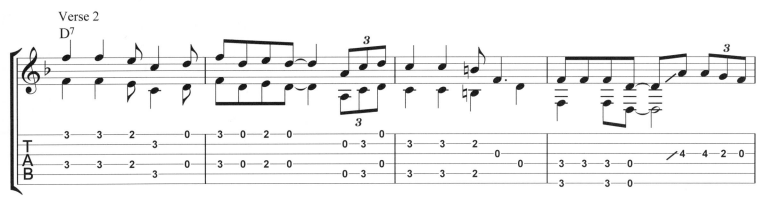

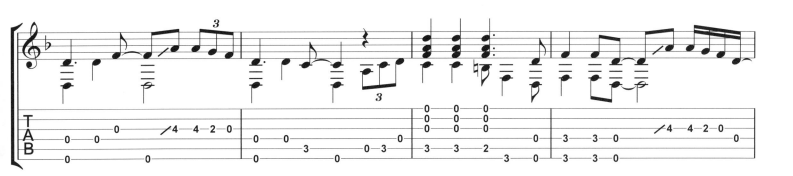

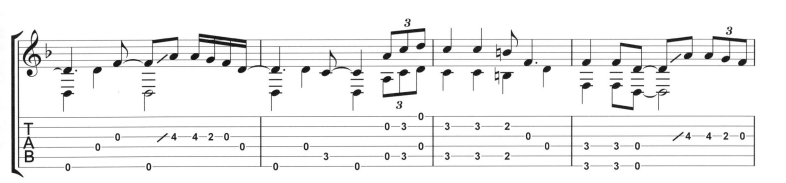

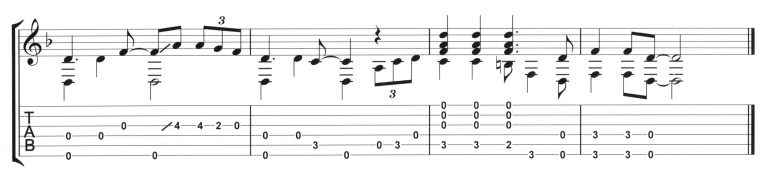

THE COMPLETE ACOUSTIC BLUES GUITAR METHOD

MISSISSIPPI MOAN

Willie Brown

Brown was born on August 6, 1900, in Clarksdale, Mississippi, a son of a sharecropper and reared on a plantation near Drew, Mississippi. From the mid-1920s until about 1930, he was the accompanying guitarist of Charley Patton, and worked with Son House during the 1930s and early 1940s. In 1930, during a record session with Patton and House for Paramount in Grafton, Wisconsin, he recorded four pieces, of which only the songs "M & O Blues" and "Future Blues" are preserved. Little is known about his final years. Brown died in 1952.

This song is a 12-bar blues in Open G tuning (D G D G B D) based on some of the playing styles of Robert Johnson, Willie Brown, and Charlie Patton. The two main techniques featured here are brushing in both the bass and treble lines, and playing chords using smaller chord forms (meaning two or three notes rather than the usual block positions). Both the bass and melody are brushed across more than one string. For example, in measures 1 through 4, brush the three melody notes with your fingers and brush the bass strings with your thumb. The goal is to attain a strum-like effect in both lines. This arrangement is a composite of the sounds and techniques of classic recordings of the Mississippi Delta players, including Charlie Patton's "Screaming" and "Hollering the Blues," as well as Robert Johnson's "Terraplane Blues."

Open G tuning:
D G D G B D

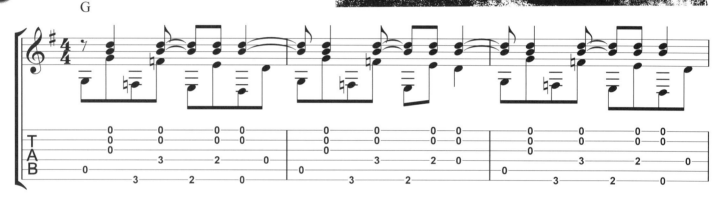

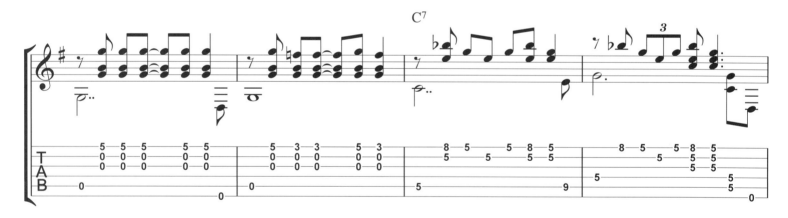

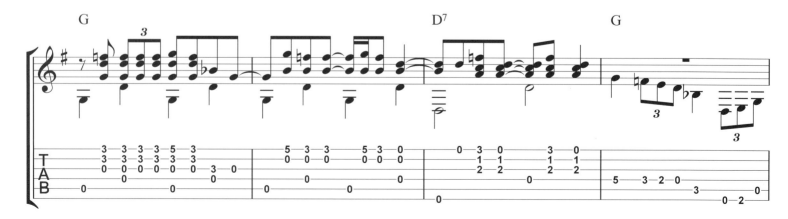

YOU GOT TO KNOW HOW

Lonnie Johnson

Alonzo (Lonnie) Johnson, born in New Orleans in 1889 or 1894, originated an unequaled style of single-string lead fingerpicking. By 1932, he had recorded 130 sides, more than any blues singer of his time. Historically, he is also seen as a bridge between blues and jazz.

"You Got to Know How" is played in the unusual (but practical) Drop DG tuning in the key of D. This is an altered Open G tuning: D G D G B E. Since the top four strings are the same as in standard tuning, and since the open bass strings play the tonic notes of the D and G chords, you have the freedom to use those chord and melodic ideas in all parts of the fingerboard without having to hold down full chord positions. Lonnie Johnson, the first blues artist to record a guitar instrumental, played in this tuning almost exclusively. "You Got to Know How" is a 12-bar blues that uses a melody played as two- or three-note chord shapes and single-string runs played out of the chord positions. For example, in measure 9, the single-string run outlines an A bar chord, and in measure 2, the two-note positions are parts of a D chord. In measures 5 and 6, the melody is based on the two-note G chord formed on frets 12 and 10. In the second verse, there are further variations of melodic riffs based on the chord positions. Lonnie Johnson's recording of "Away Down the Alley," the first recorded blues instrumental, features nine verses of his improvisational creativity.

Drop DG tuning: D G D G B E

Slow Shuffle

BLUES AIN'T GONE

"Blues Ain't Gone" features octave bass lines playing the shuffle rhythm. The unusual 14-bar structure and progression using a C minor chord gives the tune a modal, almost minor sound. The shuffle rhythm is played entirely in the bass in the G chord phrases and then shifts to the melody on the C and C minor chords. This tune is an example of the many different sounds and non–12-bar structures in country blues. I based this one on the sounds of Joe Williams, Charlie Patton and Willie Brown.

Open G tuning:
D G D G B D

Slow Shuffle

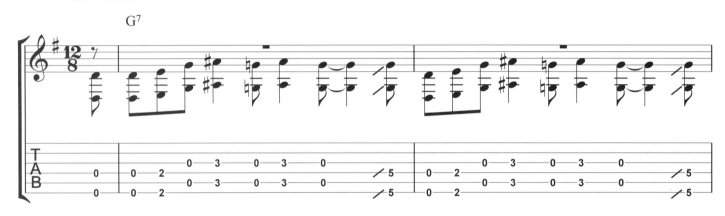

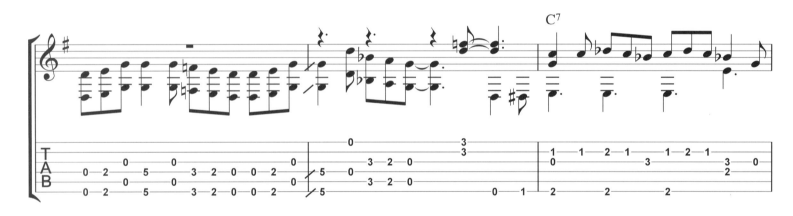

FAREWELL BABY

"Farewell Baby" is a 20-bar blues tune based on a traditional melody played by many country blues artists. This version is based on the recording by Joe Callicott. This unique tune in Drop D tuning (D A D G B E) is played with a steady alternating bass line and a melody line played out of the chord positions. There are a few tricky phrases, such as the triplets in measures 15 and 19. Also in these measures, the melody (fingers) drops below the bass part (thumb). There are variations of the D chord positions, and the G7 can be a stretch while playing the melody at the same time.

Drop D tuning:
D A D G B E

Swing ($\sqrt{}\sqrt{} = \sqrt{}^3\sqrt{}$)

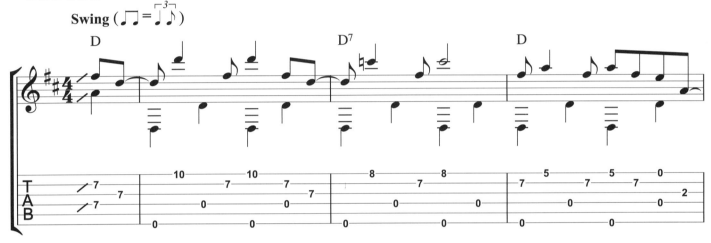

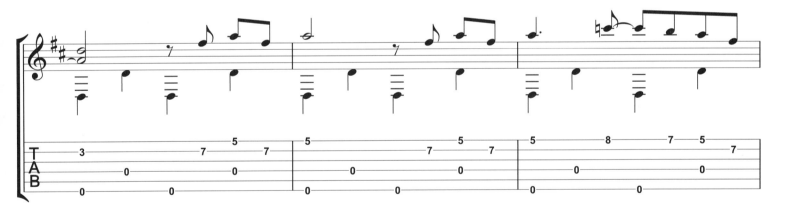

THE COMPLETE ACOUSTIC BLUES GUITAR METHOD

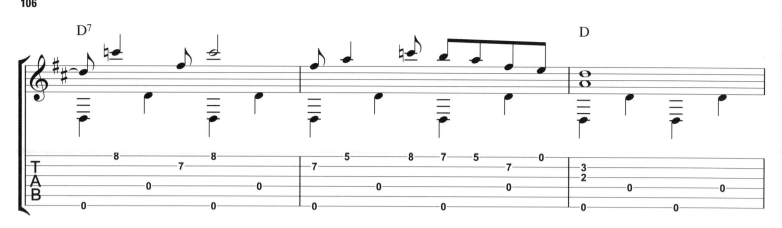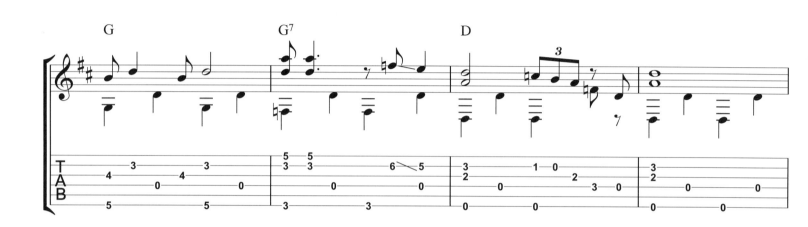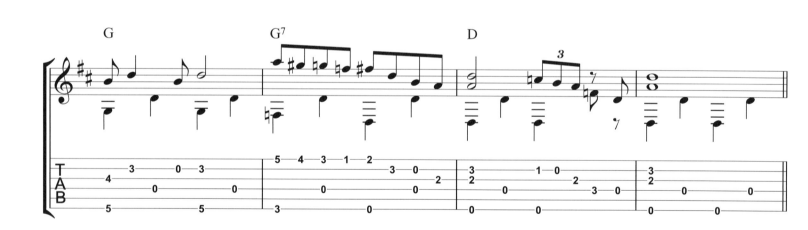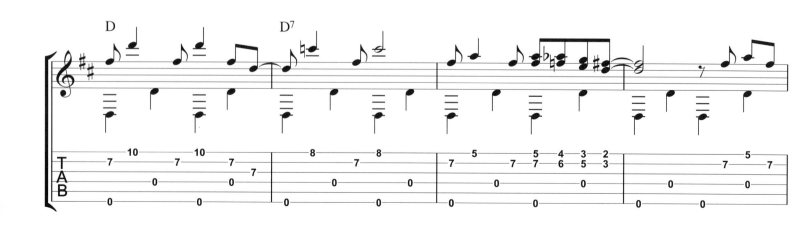

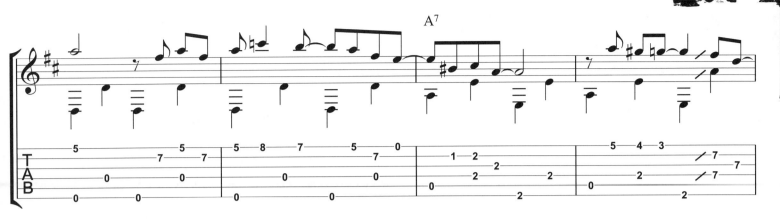
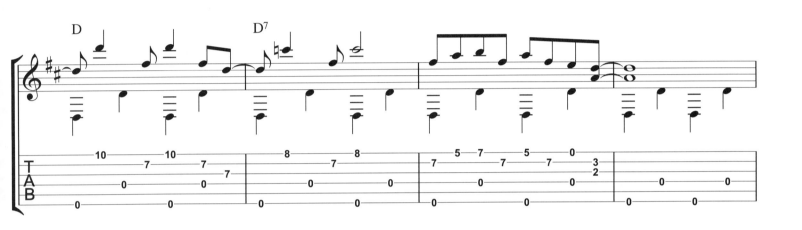
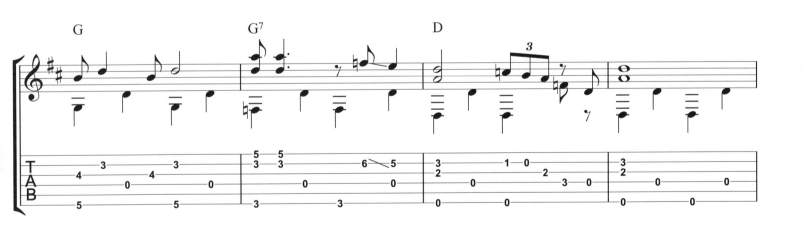
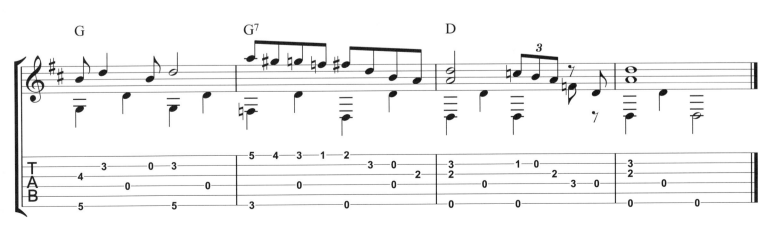

BLUES IN G

"Blues in G" is played in Drop DG (or Altered Open G) tuning in the key of G (D G D G B E). The rhythm of the tune is a slow shuffle played in the bass. In the first verse, the bass is played as a brush across two or three strings. To do this, brush your thumb across the strings in one motion. In the second verse, the bass becomes the melodic line, while the fingers are punctuating the rhythm with open strings. As in "You Got to Know How" (played in the same tuning but in the key of D), using the open bass strings of G and D in this tune makes it easier to explore melodic riffs on those chords without having to hold down full chord positions.

Drop DG tuning:
D G D G B E

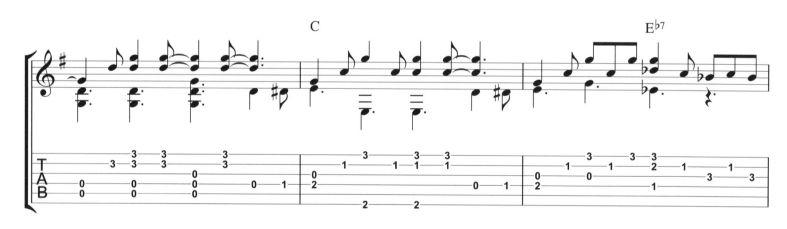

Verse 2

POLICE BLUES

"Police Blues," in Open D tuning (D A D F# A D), is based on the playing of Blind Blake's "Police Dog Blues." This arrangement also uses the most common chord positions in Open D, and the three verses illustrate the variations in both the melody and bass parts. It's worth mentioning that although Blind Blake recorded extensively, he played only one song in Open D tuning, and it was one of his greatest guitar arrangements.

Open D tuning:
D A D F# A D

JUMP BLUES

Francis "Scrapper" Blackwell

Born in Syracuse, North Carolina, in 1903, and reared in Indianapolis, Blackwell taught himself guitar in childhood. Most of his recordings were accompaniments behind the popular pianist Leroy Carr, whom he met in the late 1920s. One of the most original blues artists, Blackwell developed a singular guitar style as well as recording some of the most original sides. Although his recording career waned with Carr's death in 1935, he was still a superb guitarist when rediscovered in Indianapolis in 1959. There he was shot to death in 1962.

"Jump Blues" is one of the more difficult pieces to play in Drop D tuning (D A D G B E). The interplay of the fast rhythmic syncopation using grace notes in the bass and the quick melody riffs give the tune a unique feel. Play this one slow to get the groove. In all three chord phrases, the melody and bass bounce from one to the other. In the second verse, I wrote out some variations in both lines. "Jump Blues" is inspired by a few sources: Tommy Johnson's recording of "Canned Heat Blues," as well as some of Scrapper Blackwell and Snooks Eaglin's playing ideas.

Drop D tuning:
D A D G B E

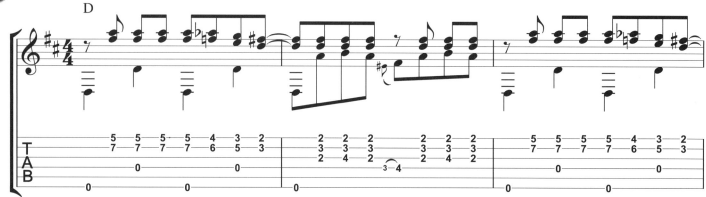

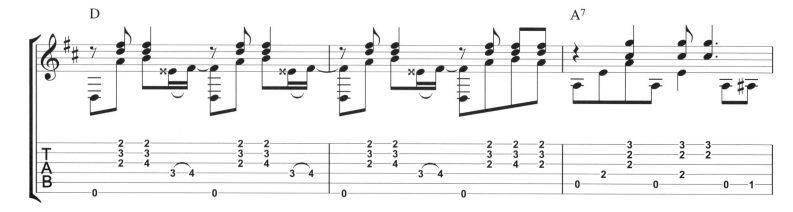

EXPANDING THE TRADITIONS

SUNDAY CHURCH MEETING

"Sunday Church Meeting" is a gospel instrumental in the style of Rev. Gary Davis's gospel playing. Using partial chords to play a melody is one technique that helped Davis to create the church-like sound of many of his guitar arrangements. Most of these chord shapes are played on the top three or four strings, and the melody is harmonized using these smaller chords to create a chord melody. Sometimes the melody weaves in and out and connects the chord shapes. Although the tune is in the key of G, it starts on a D chord.

Standard tuning

Gospel

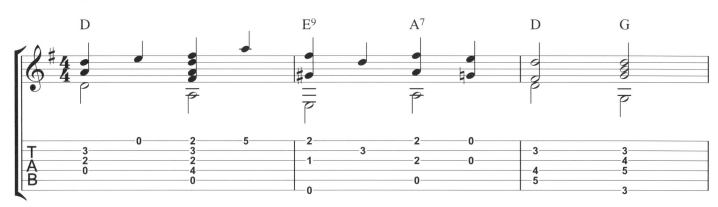

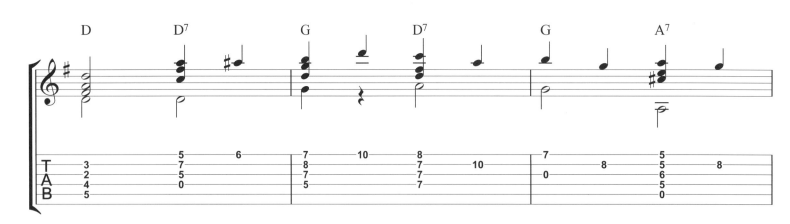

HUDSON RIVER BOOGIE

"Hudson River Boogie" is a 24-bar blues swing tune played mostly with two single-note lines running through the chord progression. Since there are no full chord positions to hold down, the bass and melody simply outline the chord shapes with one or two notes in the position. In the second part, the descending bass riffs are out of the E chord. Even though you are not playing the full chord shapes, it's a good idea to understand and "see" where they are. Although based on the ideas of traditional blues, this tune has a more modern sound to it.

Standard tuning

Medium Swing (♫ = ♪♪)

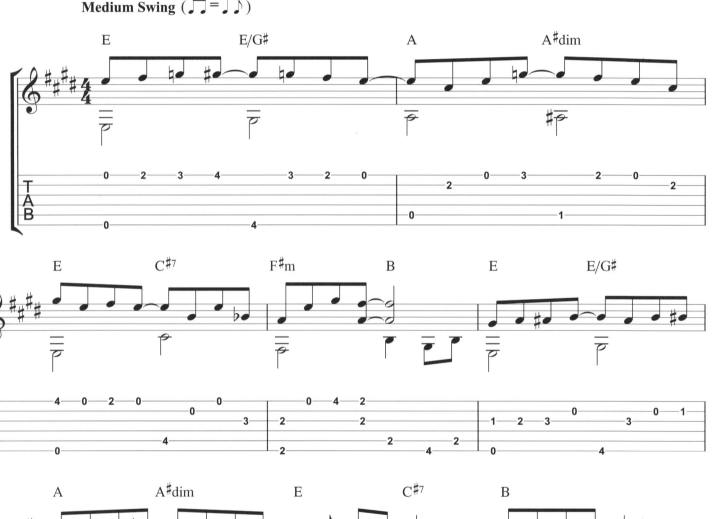

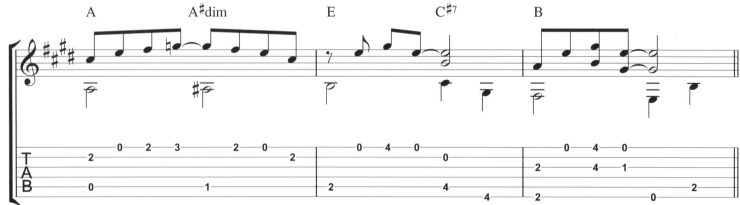

SUNSET LAKE RAG

"Sunset Lake Rag" is a composition based on the ragtime piano sounds of Scott Joplin and the classic ragtime of the early 1900s. The sound and syncopations are very different from ragtime blues players such as Blind Blake and Big Bill Broonzy, who played with a very rhythmic bass line. In this style, the bass has an easy, alternating, on-the-beat swing, but features a more complicated melody (and chord structure) syncopated against it. The form is a full 32-bar song structure in two parts. This tune is a departure in sound from the other songs in this collection, but it illustrates many of the same fingerpicking ideas while expanding the harmonic and melodic possibilities—and it's just a great fingerpicking tune.

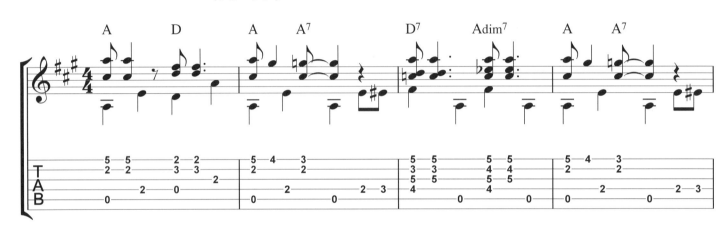

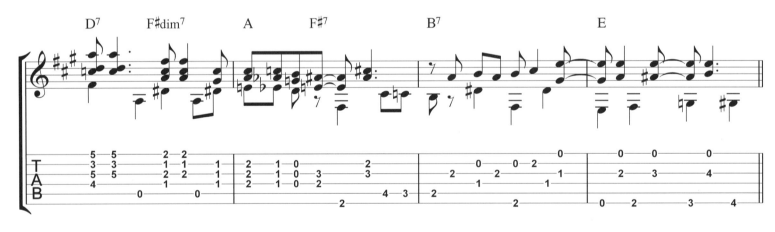

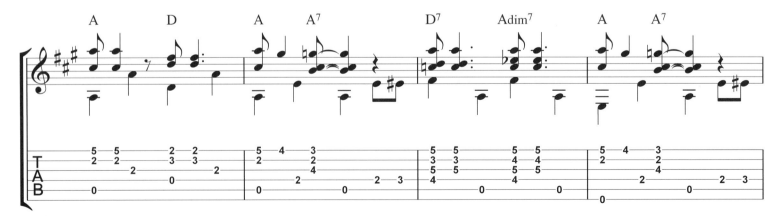

SPIRITUAL FOR R.G.D.

"Spiritual for R.G.D." is a gospel instrumental tribute to Rev. Gary Davis. The arrangement illustrates the use of various positions of the same chord to harmonize a melody. Understanding these movable smaller chords offers a simple and direct way into understanding the fretboard. The chord shapes are played on the top three or four strings.

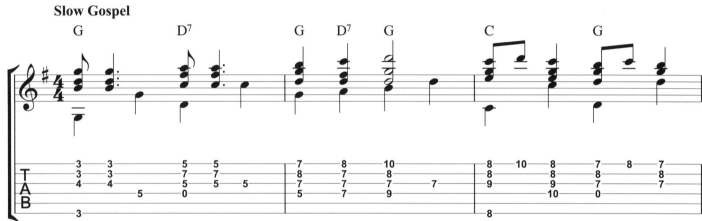

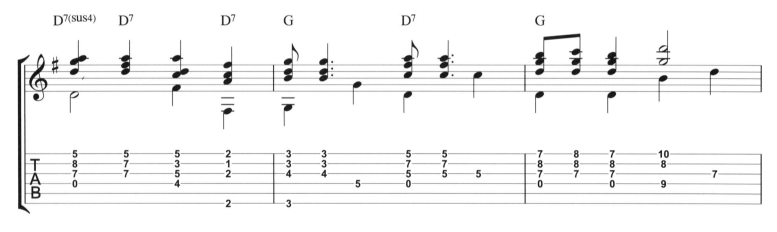

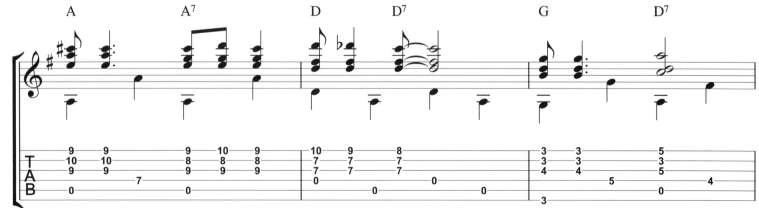

VIRGINIA STOMP

"Virginia Stomp" is another example of how the ideas of traditional blues can be used to create new fingerstyle arrangements. It is based on the chord progression and structure of "Hesitation Blues," usually played in the key of C, and arranged around the ideas in the key of G. It uses a lot of syncopation and new chord shapes. The E♭7 chord is played in the first position, bars 21 and 22 (in the second verse) have a long finger stretch, and the D chord phrase is played only in the melody. To help you feel the bounce and groove of this tune, I would suggest accenting the bass part throughout.

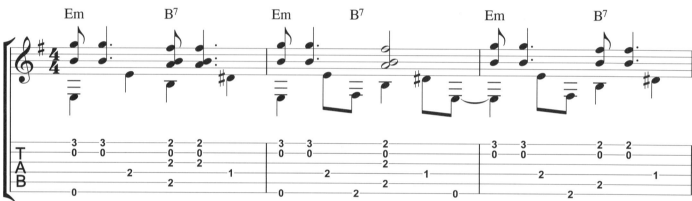

AT MIDNIGHT

"At Midnight" is a 22-bar riff tune played in Open D tuning (D A D F♯ A D). The main riff is a chromatic melody played on top of a steady bass. Along with using the G minor chord and the open structure, the tune has a modal, or minor, sound to it. The modal feel is created because the progression stays on a D tonality (chord) without hitting the open third string (the note F♯), and the melody weaves chromatically through the chord. In the first few bars, the first downbeat of each measure is tied to the previous measure, creating the rhythmic groove against which the riffs are played. I based this arrangement of the sounds and ideas of Skip James's playing in Open D Minor tuning.

Open D tuning:
D A D F♯ A D

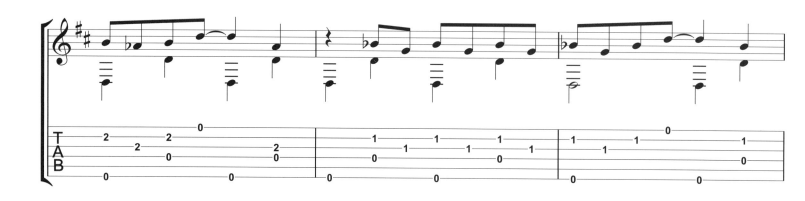

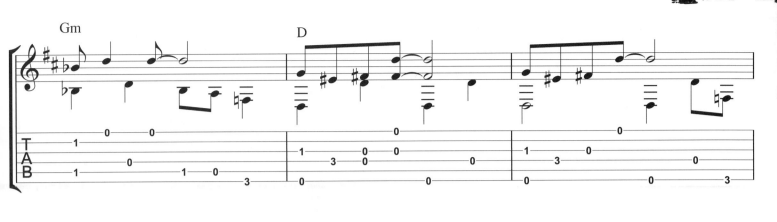

DELTA NIGHTS

Son House

Eddie James "Son" House was born in Clarksdale, Mississippi, in 1920. Unlike so many other blues guitarists who turned from secular to religious music later in life, Son House began his musical career completely devoted to church music until his mid-twenties, at which point he let loose with a driving delta blues style that inspired Robert Johnson, Charley Patton and Willie Brown. Son's career had several interruptions including a two-year stretch in jail for shooting and killing a man. (The sentence was commuted after judicial review). His recording career was sporadic, but extensive.

"Delta Nights" is based on a popular melody recorded by many musicians, including Son House and Skip James. This is an updated arrangement of "Four O'Clock Blues" that I heard Son House play and subsequently recorded with him. Each verse harmonizes the melody in various ways, using notes in the chord positions. There is no pattern to the picking, only the church-like cadences of each phrase and the different ways the melody weaves in and out of the chords.

He recorded several sides for Alan Lomax on the Library of Congress series in the mid-1940s, and fell into obscurity until the folk-blues revival of the 1960s when he was regularly featured at major festivals in the U.S. and in Europe. Among his best known tunes are "Death Letter Blues" and "See That My Grave Is Kept Clean." Son House died in 1988.